MATLAB®

for Behavioral Scientists

Titles of Related Interest from Lawrence Erlbaum

Cindy S. Bergeman (Ed.) and Steven M. Boker (Ed.): *Methodological Issues in Aging Research*

Steven M. Boker (Ed.) and Michael J. Wenger (Ed.): *Data Analytic Techniques for Dynamical Systems*

Barbara Byrne: *Structural Equation Modeling With EQS Basic Concepts, Applications, and Programming (2nd Edition)*

Rudolf N. Cardinal and Michael R. F. Aitken: *ANOVA for the Behavioural Sciences Researcher*

Jacob Cohen, Patricia Cohen, Stephen G. West and Leona S. Aiken: *Applied Multiple Regression/Correlation Analysis for the Behavioral Sciences (3rd Edition)*

Steven M. Downing (Ed.) and Thomas M. Haladyna (Ed.): *Handbook of Test Development*

Judith L. Green (Ed.), Gregory Camilli (Ed.) and Patricia B. Elmore (Ed.): *Handbook of Complementary Methods in Education Research (3rd Edition)*

Nancy L. Leech, Karen C. Barrett and George A. Morgan: *SPSS for Intermediate Statistics Use and Interpretation (2nd Edition)*

Richard G. Lomax: *An Introduction to Statistical Concepts for Education and the Behavioral Sciences (2nd Edition)*

Scott E. Maxwell and Harold D. Delaney: *Designing Experiments and Analyzing Data A Model Comparison Perspective (2nd Edition)*

George A. Morgan, Nancy L. Leech, Gene W. Gloeckner and Karen C. Barrett: *SPSS for Introductory Statistics Use and Interpretation (3rd Edition)*

Tenko Raykov and George A. Marcoulides: *A First Course in Structural Equation Modeling (2nd Edition)*

Timothy C. Urdan: *Statistics in Plain English (2nd Edition)*

MATLAB®

for Behavioral Scientists

David A. Rosenbaum
Pennsylvania State University

Psychology Press
Taylor & Francis Group

New York   London

Cover design by Kathryn Houghtaling Lacey

Cover art generated with MATLAB by Robrecht van der Wel (see pp. 213–216)

Library of Congress Cataloging-in-Publication Data

Rosenbaum, David A. MATLAB for behavioral scientists / David A. Rosenbaum.
      p. cm.
Includes bibliographical references and index.
ISBN 978-0-8058-6227-0 — 0-8058-6227-7 (cloth)
ISBN 978-0-8058-6319-2 — 0-8058-6319-2 (pbk.)
ISBN 978-1-4106-1611-1 — 1-4106-1911-8 (e book)
1. Psychology—Data processing. 2. MATLAB.   I. Title.
BF39.5.R67   2007
150.285'5133—dc22   2006031827
                                                CIP

Books published by Lawrence Erlbaum Associates are printed on acid-free paper, and their bindings are chosen for strength and durability.

Printed in the United States of America
10 9 8 7 6 5 4 3 2

This book is dedicated to the students of PSY 525
(Spring 2006, Penn State University, University Park),
shown here along with the author.
From left to right: Robrecht van der Wel, Adam Christensen,
Andy Lee, Matt Walsh, Myro Olida, Joe Santamaria,
Matt Gaydos, Vera Pawlowski, Rajal Cohen, Aaron Mitchel,
David Rosenbaum, Mohamed Tlili, Elisabeth Hein,
Mei-Hua Lee, Tyler Phelps, Rose Halterman,
Rebecca Von Der Heide, Jen Bittner, and Brie Sullivan.
Not shown: Brad Fesi.

Brief Contents

Contents

Preface

Behavioral scientists use computers in virtually all their work—in data collection, in data analysis, in data presentation, and in data simulation. Yet, as far as I know, there is no book written specifically for behavioral scientists on how to program with a general-purpose programming language. Why there is no such book is a matter for speculation. One reason may be that behavioral scientists have generally relied on applications generated by others. Another may be that computer programming has been viewed as the province of engineers and other practitioners of "hard science."

I believe that computer programming is not too hard for behavioral scientists. On the contrary, I am convinced that if computer programming is presented in terms that are relevant to the concerns of behavioral scientists, they can quickly and easily learn to program for themselves.

Knowing how to program is tremendously valuable. It allows you to dig into problems you are studying and frees you to do whatever you want, computationally speaking. Having this intellectual freedom can be professionally liberating as well. It is helpful not to have to rely on the kindness of strangers to get your work done. To the extent that programming requires clarity of thought, learning how to program can help you think, write, and speak more clearly than you already do.

Learning to program also "builds character" in the sense that you may think you have a clear idea of what your program should do, but you may inadvertently make mistakes that cause the program not to run, generate unexpected results, or produce results that seem reasonable at first but then turn out to be flawed. Conceiving, writing, and debugging computer programs can be a humbling experience. This is the character-building part of programming. There is also a joyful part of programming. When you see your program work, especially if your program can do something that has not been done before, you can feel justly proud of the achievement.

Why is the computer programming language introduced here MATLAB? MATLAB (short for Matrix Laboratory), is a commercial product of a company called The MathWorks (Natick Massachusetts). I do not work for this company and have no commercial connection with them, so the following can be taken as my honest opinion of their product: MATLAB is a simple yet powerful language for computer programming. It has an active community of users who are engaged in many branches of science and engineering. One of MATLAB's most attractive features is that it offers high-level commands for performing calculations with large, as well as small, data sets and for generating publication-quality graphics. Another attraction is that MATLAB allows you to present stimuli and gather responses with precise timing. Yet another attraction is that MATLAB is platform-independent. For these reasons and others, MATLAB is a good language for behavioral scientists. A growing number of behavioral scientists have learned MATLAB and are using it actively, drawing upon and in turn contributing to the shared programming experience of investigators in other fields. This state of affairs suggests that more and more behavioral scientists will want to learn MATLAB in the future. This book is designed to help them do so.

Perhaps the biggest drawback of MATLAB is that it has not been documented as well as one would like. Those behavioral scientists who have learned MATLAB are intrepid souls who have made their way through sometimes labyrinthine manuals or other complex sources of information that accompany MATLAB or are available elsewhere (in books and on web sites). Virtually all such information is designed for people with considerable technical training in mathematics and engineering, not to mention prior programming experience. MATLAB has not yet been presented for those who are new to programming, nor for those with the relatively minimal quantitative training that, for better or worse, characterizes the knowledge base of many people in behavioral science.

My aim in preparing this book has been to offer an introduction to MATLAB that respects these limitations while also appreciating the special programming needs that behavioral scientists have—some of which are very challenging (e.g., dealing with messy data or creating data gathering protocols that are "idiot-proof"). I have tried to prepare this book in a way that lets those without much training in mathematics or engineering take advantage of MATLAB's capabilities. One advantage of this approach is that MATLAB can provide a friendly environment in which to explore more technical material than many behavioral scientists are acquainted with.

To make the material as accessible as possible, I have tried to make the text as user-friendly as I could. One way I have done this is to use an example-based approach, illustrating each new principle with one or more illustrations of usable code. Another way is to start each chapter with a list of things you may want to do, followed by commands you will probably need to do those things. These start-of-chapter lists will allow you to use this book as a reference source once you understand the basics of MATLAB. Thus, after you have worked your way through the book, you can later turn to a section of interest and quickly get the detailed information you need to complete the programming task you are working on. So if you want to plot data in three dimensions, for example, you will be able to turn to the first page of Chapter 11, Three Dimensional Graphics, note that this chapter has a section (Section 11.2) on plotting in three dimensions, and then be reminded that the special command associated with this topic is "plot3," as indicated in the list of commands below the section headings. You can then either use that command in the program you are writing or turn to Section 11.2 to find code you can adapt for your own purposes.

A third way I have tried to make the text as user-friendly as possible is to work with the publisher of this book to put the programs and code output on a website: www.matlab-behave.com. On this website you will be able to find and copy the programs and program outputs in this volume. The program outputs on the website have color, whereas those modalities are absent from this book.

Readers are often curious about their authors, so here's a little bit about me. I am a cognitive psychologist with a PhD. in Experimental Psychology from Stanford University (1977). I became attracted to cognitive psychology as an undergraduate at Swarthmore College, which I attended from 1970–1973. My fascination with cognitive psychology led me to graduate school, where I completed my PhD in 1977 under the supervision of Roger Shepard and Gordon Bower. I then worked at Bell Labs (Murray Hill, NJ) in Saul Sternberg's Human Information Processing Research department, after which I taught at Hampshire College

(Amherst, MA), at the University of Massachusetts (Amherst), and at the Pennsylvania State University (University Park), where I have been on the faculty since 1994. Between 2000 and 2005, I was the Editor of the *Journal of Experimental Psychology: Human Perception and Performance*, a publication of the American Psychological Association.

This book grew out of a graduate seminar I taught in Penn State's Psychology Department in the Spring of 2004 and again in the Spring of 2006. When I first advertised the course, emphasizing that it, like this book, was meant for students with no prior programming experience, I was amazed by the level of interest. The course was oversubscribed, with a large number of graduate students, undergraduate students, and even several faculty members wanting to participate. These people wanted to learn how to program, knowing that programming would be a valuable skill for their careers. They also jumped at the chance to learn to program in a behavioral science context, where the examples would be relevant to their interests and the material would be pitched at a level with which they would be comfortable. MATLAB was known to be widely used at our university. Every public computer lab at Penn State (open to all Penn State students, faculty, and staff), has MATLAB. The course notes from the seminar I taught for the students in the first run of the seminar evolved into this book, which is the book I wish I had when I was learning MATLAB myself.

A number of individuals played a valuable role in the conception, completion, and refinement of this work. Mike Blaguszewski, my teaching assistant in the Spring 2004 seminar, helped both me and the students of that seminar by translating often inscrutable computer manuals into terms we could understand. Rajal Cohen, my teaching assistant in the Spring 2006 seminar, was also a wonderful aide, particularly in the way she carefully checked each chapter of this book. She provided me with many valuable suggestions about the text, for which I am deeply indebted. Jason Augustyn, Rajal Cohen, Amanda Dawson, Rick Gilmore, Elisabeth Hein, Frouke Hermens, Steve Jax, Ruud Meulenbroek, and Jonathan Vaughan helped me hone my MATLAB programming skills in our lab work together. Volker Franz, Antonia Hamilton, Hank Heijank, Erik Reichle, and Jonathan Vaughan provided valuable comments on earlier drafts of this work. Judith Kroll, my wife of 30 years at the time of this writing, brought me back to reality when my mind's eye was filled with computer code at the dinner table. More importantly, in her role as a full and equal partner in our marriage (she is also a professor at Penn State), she helped me think more clearly and constructively than I might have done otherwise. Any errors that remain in the book are mine, not those of people at The MathWorks, my friends, students, or colleagues, or, most assuredly, my wife's.

A final word of thanks goes to the people at Lawrence Erlbaum Associates. I decided to sign with LEA partly because Lori Stone Handelman so impressed me with her verve and dedication. The editorial team that handled production of the volume, led by Steve Rutter, Tony Messina, and Providence Rao was very helpful.

A final word about why I decided to sign with LEA was that Larry Erlbaum has done a great service to the field of cognitive psychology, being one of its most stalwart publishers over several decades. It is fitting that this book about the use of computer programming in behavioral science—the first such book—be published by a company that was founded by an individual who has helped usher behavioral science into the modern age.

—*David A. Rosenbaum*

1. Introduction

This chapter covers the following topics:

1.1   Getting Oriented

Computers are vital to every branch of science today, including behavioral science. Whether behavioral scientists use computers to obtain responses in questionnaires, present visual stimuli, display brain images, or generate data graphs, their ability to make strides in their research depends to a large extent on the ability to use computers effectively.

Many specialized computer packages let behavioral scientists do their work, and each one takes some time to learn. It is useful to know how to use these specialized packages, but it is also tantalizing to consider the possibility of learning how to program for yourself, because all specialized computer packages rely on underlying code, and knowing how to generate such code can allow you to be self-sufficient, or nearly so, in your own research.

Suppose, for example, that you want to develop a mathematical model of some cognitive process. It is convenient to be able to write a program that lets you explore the mathematical model freely, seeing the results that can be obtained with different equations, different parameter values, and so on. Similarly, rather than having to analyze data in ways that would be cumbersome with existing spreadsheet applications, it is refreshing to be able to write the analysis program to your own specifications. As one more example, when viewing graphs of obtained or theoretical data in a variety of forms, it is gratifying to be able to generate those graphs quickly and easily.

The computer language introduced here, MATLAB, provides you with these capabilities. MATLAB is available from The Mathworks (www.mathworks.com), a company with which I have no affiliation. MATLAB has become popular in several branches of engineering and science, including behavioral science. Nonetheless, to the best of my knowledge no book has appeared about MATLAB for behavioral scientists. Nor, for that matter, has a book come out

1

for behavioral scientists about any other general-purpose programming language. It is high time for such a volume, which is why I have taken the time to prepare this one.

Will it be worth your time to read this book? Once you have gone through the text and generated your own MATLAB programs based on the material presented here you should have enough programming skill to do most of what you need to for your own behavioral research needs. You will at least know how to get the extra information that will enable you to do so.

This book will be most useful to you if you use it in two stages. In the first stage, go through the parts of the book that are most relevant to your needs. Go through these parts in considerable detail, working problems and developing the hands-on skills that will make you a MATLAB user, not just a MATLAB appreciator. In the second stage, rely on the book as a reference, turning quickly to the sections that provide examples adaptable to your programming needs.

To make the book as useful as possible as a reference source, I have designed it so you can find the examples you need quickly and easily. Turn to the opening page of any chapter for a list of things you may want to do. Beneath that list is a list of associated commands. The text provides examples you can adapt for your own purposes. Those examples can be copied by hand into your own programs or you can copy and paste them from the web site associated with this book (www.matlab-behave.com), where the programs and their outputs are available.

1.2 Getting an Overview of This Book

Acquiring a new skill such as computer programming can be daunting. It helps to have an overview of what you can expect as you pursue this path. Here is a road map of the contents of this book, along with explanations of the goals of each chapter:

1. **Introduction.** By reading the present chapter, you will learn more than you may already know about how computers work and what computer programming languages do. You will also learn about how you should approach computer programming. Finally, by reading this chapter, you will understand how this book is organized. That information should help you use the book efficiently.

2. **Interacting with MATLAB.** By delving into the second chapter, you will learn how to activate MATLAB's windows to open, edit, save, and run MATLAB programs.

3. **Matrices.** By studying the third chapter, you will understand how MATLAB enables you to store and access data. Briefly, MATLAB lets you store data in matrices consisting of one or more rows and one or more columns. Matrices are so fundamental to MATLAB that the name of the language is actually short for "Matrix Laboratory."

4. **Calculations.** Computers are very good at calculating. Chapter 4 shows how to get your computer to carry out the calculations you want using MATLAB.

5. **Contingencies.** One of the main purposes of a computer program is to perform different actions depending on existing conditions. Chapter 5 shows you how to exploit such contingencies with MATLAB.

6. **Input–Output.** Chapter 6 shows you how to control your computer's interactions with the external world. You will learn to design programs that let you create dialogs

with users (including participants in behavioral studies), and to read and write data to and from external files.

7. **Data Types.** One of the most convenient features of MATLAB is that it frees you from the need to declare the types of your variables. This statement may not mean very much if you have not programmed before, so you will have to take my word for it that it can be liberating to be freed from the need to explicitly declare what type of data every one of your variables is. On the other hand, it is useful to understand what data types are available in MATLAB so you can declare or otherwise format your data types accordingly. Relevant information is given in Chapter 7.

8. **Modules and Functions.** Chapter 8 shows you how to write programs as stand-alone modules and functions. Such modules and functions can be called by a variety of programs. Using modules and functions can help you approach programming from a top-down as well as a bottom-up perspective.

9. **Plots.** Chapter 9 is the first of four chapters on graphics (widely regarded as one of the special strengths of MATLAB). Chapter 9 shows you how to make line graphs, bar graphs, and other sorts of graphs suitable for professional presentations and publications.

10. **Lines, Shapes, and Images.** Chapter 10 shows you how to create, import, or reshape lines, shapes, and other images that can either stand alone or be included in graphs.

11. **Three-Dimensional Graphics.** Chapter 11 takes you from two-dimensional graphics to graphing in three dimensions.

12. **Animations.** Chapter 12 moves from static graphics to movies.

13. **Sounds.** Chapter 13 introduces you to the control of auditory stimuli.

14. **Going On.** Chapter 14 provides you with pointers for going on with MATLAB. Here you will get exposure to graphical user interfaces (GUIs), other capabilities that MATLAB affords, and third-party applications that may be of use to you (e.g., PsychToolbox).

A lot of material will be covered in this book. Are all of the chapters necessary for you? If you have no need to play sounds, show animations, or generate three-dimensional graphics, you may safely ignore chapters 10–13. However, leafing through these chapters may help you overcome any prejudices you might have against these topics. At the same time, there are chapters you can't avoid, unless you want to emerge from this book the way Woody Allen emerged from his speed-reading of Tolstoy's epic novel, *War and Peace*: "It was about Russia," Woody Allen said in one of his comedies. The truly essential chapters of this book are chapters 2–5. You simply cannot go on to the later chapters and expect to have control of your programs if you don't have command of the material in chapters 2–5. The only way to gain that command is to work your way slowly and carefully through the examples and exercises in these chapters.

When you write your own programs, how will you know if your programs are correct? The MATLAB programming environment introduced in Chapter 2 serves as an excellent source of feedback as you write and then run your own programs. You will be told, indirectly or directly, if your syntax (word use and punctuation) is acceptable or unacceptable. If your syntax is unacceptable, you will get an error message. Otherwise, your program will run. If you get an error message, it will be up to you to figure out what change needs to be made to resolve the error. It takes some time to learn to interpret error messages, but over time you will learn to do so.

If your syntax is acceptable, it will be up to you to decide whether the output you get is correct. Judging the correctness of your program's output is often as challenging as generating acceptable syntax. Sometimes a program seems to work but a subtle error lurking behind it makes the output wrong. Detecting such mistakes is one of the most challenging aspects of programming. In general, developing a program that works correctly requires more than an understanding of programming syntax. It also requires greater clarity and explicitness about the procedures to be followed than is required in everyday life. Striving for such clarity and explicitness is one of the things that makes programming a humbling experience. However, learning to develop well-crafted computer programs is worth the effort.

1.3 Understanding Computer Architecture

As a first step toward learning to program, it helps to learn about computer architecture. Knowing the main components of computers will help you understand what features of the environment your program must deal with.

All working computers have five basic elements. As shown in Figure 1.2.1, these are: (a) input devices (keyboards, mice, microphones, etc.); (b) output devices (screens, printers, loudspeakers, etc.); (c) storage devices (hard disks, floppy disks, DVDs, etc.); (d) primary memory; and (e) the central processing unit. The first three components should need no further explanation. The last two components merit more discussion.

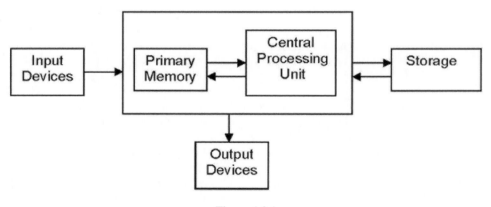

Figure 1.2.1

Primary memory (Item 4 on the list) is like human or animal working memory. Its contents are currently active information. The amount of information that can be kept in this active state is limited in biological agents (humans and animals) and in computers. The amount of information a computer can maintain in primary memory is hardware dependent.

Because the capacity of primary memory is limited, it is important to be mindful of the amount of information a computer can keep active at a given time. The amount of information made active by a program such as one written in MATLAB depends on the number of variables that are declared and the number of bits (the number of 1s and 0s) associated with each variable. Essentially, there are three ways of using primary memory efficiently: (a) defining just the variables that are needed; (b) clearing variables once they are no longer needed; and (c) defining the types of the variables such that the amount of information used by them is no larger than needed. We return to these topics in Chapter 7 (Data Types).

Returning to the components of computer architecture, the fifth is the central processing unit. This is the part of the computer that carries out instructions. For present purposes, the central processing unit, or CPU, can be likened to consciousness. Conciousness, it is said (James, 1890), can only occupy one thought at a time. The same can be said of a computer's CPU. It can only handle one instruction at a time, at least in a conventional digital computer of the sort used by MATLAB. Handling just one instruction at a time is called *serial* processing. Handling more than one instruction at a time is called *parallel* processing.

Serial processing can occur at high rates on modern computers. For example, the computer on which this text was prepared (a Dell™ laptop) runs at 2 gigahertz (2 billion cycles per second). Regardless of the speed at which a CPU runs, however, serial processing imposes constraints on the kinds of programs one can run and therefore write in MATLAB. Suppose, for example, that you want to find the largest value among a set of values. Parallel processing is a natural way to solve this problem. If the values are shown as presented in Figure 1.2.2, for example, a brief glance at the bars lets you pick out the biggest one. The tallest bar just seems to jump out. Once it does, you can look down to find the associated element (Element 3 in this case) or you can look to the left to find the largest value (38 or so in this case).

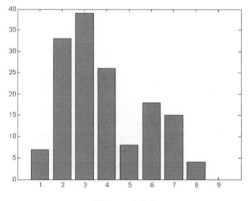

Figure 1.2.2

You might object to the fact that parallel evaluation of the heights of all the bars in this case is not actually possible, and even if it is for this particular figure, it won't be for all other figures, such as those whose largest bars have similar heights. Furthermore, you may say that the method outlined previously is not a truly parallel process because distinct stages are associated with looking down the tallest bar and looking sidewise from the top of the tallest bar. These objections are germane, considering that serial processing is inescapable in MATLAB, at least in a program that uses MATLAB in its present incarnation. To sort values or to do anything else in MATLAB, everything must be done one step at a time (serially). Knowing this can help you approach the task of programming in ways that will help you get your programs to work effectively.

1.4   Approaching the Task of Programming

How should you approach the task of programming? In my own experience, I have come to believe in the following principles.

1. Decide if a program is actually needed and if so whether you should write it.

2. Be as clear as possible about what your program should do.

3. Work incrementally.

4. Be open to negative feedback.

5. Write concise programs.

6. Write clear programs.

Let's consider each of these principles in turn.

1.5   Deciding Whether a Program Is Needed and If You Should Write It

The first principle is less obvious than you might imagine. Consider the problem discussed previously: finding the largest of a set of values. The numbers corresponding to the bars in the figure are as follows:

$$7 \quad 33 \quad 39 \quad 26 \quad 8 \quad 18 \quad 15 \quad 4 \quad 0.$$

Do you need a computer program to find the largest of these values? Obviously not. You know that the largest of these numbers is 39 and that this largest number occupies the third slot in the cue. If you only had to find the largest value in this particular arrays, you would be foolish to write a program for this task, except as an exercise. On the other hand, if you were quite sure you would often need to find the largest number in a great many array of uncertain composition, then writing a program would make more sense. A program is useful, then, for performing a well-defined task that would be too taxing to perform by hand.

The second part of Principle 1 also deserves comment. If you decide you need a program, it may or may not make sense for you to write the program yourself. Why should you write a program for a task, you may ask, if someone else has done so before?

My answer to this question is analogous to the answer given by some math teachers to the question, Why should we prove this theorem if it is been proven before? Practice makes perfect, teachers say, and even if true perfection is beyond your reach, practice will increase the chance you may someday prove something new yourself.

My view of programming is the same. You may be able to locate programs that already do things you need to do, and it may make sense for you to use those programs, especially for problems that seem very complicated or that are otherwise beyond your technical ability. On the other hand, the more practice you get in programming, the more likely it will be that you will be able to generate programs that either solve new problems or solve old problems in new ways.

1.6   Being as Clear as Possible About What Your Program Should Do

If you decide that you need a program and that you should write the program yourself (or edit a program that you or someone else has written), you will need to be as clear as possible about what your program should do. This is easier said than done. Thinking through the workings of a program can be one of the hardest aspects of programming, even harder in some cases than getting the syntax right.

Let's return to the problem of finding the largest value in an array of values. Earlier, I said that this problem cannot be solved with parallel processing but instead must be solved through serial processing. I can tell you now that MATLAB provides a program (or more precisely, a *function*), called `max`, which lets you find the maximum of a set of values (see Chapter 4). You can use this function to get the largest value in a matrix without having to reinvent the function yourself. Nevertheless, as argued earlier, it is worth thinking through how you would identify the largest value in an array. Working through this example, no matter how simple it may seem, will help you begin to think programmatically.

To think through what a program must do in order to find the largest value in an array, imagine that you have a column of numbers before you and that you can only see one of the numbers at a time, say, by sliding a card down the column. Under this circumstance, you can determine the largest value by finding the largest value *so far*. You can determine that value by assigning some very small value to a variable called, for instance, `Largest_Value_So_Far`. Then, proceeding down the list, every time you encounter a value larger than `Largest_Value_So_Far`, you can reset `Largest_Value_So_Far` to that value. After you have evaluated the last item on the list, `Largest_Value_So_Far` will be the largest of all the values.

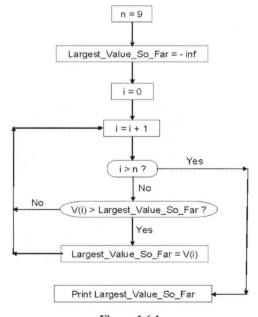

Figure 1.6.1

Figure 1.6.1 presents a flow chart for the procedure I just described, along with some other items that are needed to get the job done. One of these other items is telling the program how many values there are in the list. In this instance, there are `n = 9` values. Another item is initializing `Largest_Value_So_Far` to a particular very small value, namely, minus infinity (which can be expressed in MATLAB as `_inf`). The third item is providing an index, `i`, for each successively encountered value. An index for a value is the position of the value in the matrix it occupies. For the first item, `i = 1`, for the second item, `i = 2`, and so forth. At first, `i` is set to 0. Then `i` is incremented by 1. Value `i` of `V`, denoted `V(i)`, is assigned to `Largest_Value_So_Far` if `V(i)` is larger than `Largest_Value_So_Far` and if `i` is not greater than n. If `i` is larger than n, `Largest_Value_So_Far` is printed out.

A flowchart like this can serve as the conceptual foundation for the code to make a computer find the largest value in an array. However, you don't have to draw a flowchart before you write MATLAB code. Some people only imagine flowcharts or the steps corresponding to them. Drawing flowcharts in your head obviously gets easier as you get more and more practice with programming. In the beginning, however, it is advisable to sketch the steps your programs will follow.

How do you come up with a flowchart or its corresponding steps in the first place? The honest answer is that no one knows. Anyone who could give the answer would, in effect, know how thoughts originate, and no one at this time really has a clue about that. (If you solve this problem, a Nobel Prize awaits you.)

I can, however, offer some practical advice about how to come up with the procedures for computer programs. My main advice is to talk out loud as you imagine yourself doing the task you wish to program. Talking out loud may enable you to make explicit whatever implicit knowledge you bring to bear as you do the task. Hearing your own words will also help you identify those things you're not clear about. If you hear yourself say, "OK, next I'll somehow figure out which of the values might be OK based on some criterion I can't quite articulate but I have a vague feeling about," then you're not quite ready to write all the code you'll need.

"I think you should be more explicit here in step two."

Figure 1.6.2

Ultimately, you will need to be completely explicit about the instructions your programs contain. Relying on a miracle, as in Figure 1.6.2, just won't work, and the reason, just to be explicit, is that computers, for all their speed, are completely ignorant. They do exactly and only what they are told to do. This is one way in which programming is very different from other forms of communication. When you speak to other people, you assume, usually correctly, that they have some knowledge that lets them fill in missing information. Not so with computers, or at least conventional computers that are given new stand-alone programs. Writing successful computer programs requires a degree of explicitness that is unparalleled in other aspects of human experience. This is one reason that learning to write computer programs can be very challenging. On the other hand, being explicit to the point that a computer can carry out instructions sometimes carries over well to dealings with other people (e.g., working out ahead of time who will be a co-author of a paper describing a project that is just being started).

1.7   Working Incrementally

Another challenge associated with programming is translating your procedural ideas into language the computer can understand. Here it is useful to work incrementally. By this I mean you should build your program a little at a time, making sure each part works before you go on to another part that depends on what you've just written. You should build your program the way a reliable contractor builds a house, by making sure the foundation is solid before the basement is added, by making sure the basement is solid before the first floor is added, and so forth.

When you are reasonably sure your program works and before you add another component or make other significant changes, save the working program with a file name unique to the last working version. The moment you prepare to make changes to the program, save the file with a new name or version number before putting in any changes. Follow the American folk adage, "If it ain't broke, don't fix it." Remember that computer storage is cheap. There is no harm in having a folder full of documents called `Max_Program_01.m`, `Max_Program_02.m`, `Max_Program_03.m`, and so on. It may be that the version you'll use for actual work is `Max_Program_101.m`. There is nothing wrong with this. (The Microsoft Word file I submitted to the publisher for this particular chapter was named `Intro_232.doc`. In other words, the version of this chapter that I submitted was the 232nd. Many versions were only slight updates of their predecessors.)

1.8   Being Open to Negative Feedback

How can you tell if your program works? As you consider this question, one attitude should rule over all others: *Be open to negative feedback*. If you treat negative feedback as a help rather than as a hindrance, you will become a better, and certainly happier, programmer than if you treat negative feedback in a negative way.

The research of psychologists Carol Dweck and Janine Bempechat (1983) is relevant here. Dweck and Bempechat distinguished between people who take negative feedback as signs of their lack of talent (*entity* learners), and people who treat negative feedback as cues for ways to improve their performance (*incremental* learners). When you program, it is important to have the attitude of an incremental learner rather than an entity learner. You will learn much more if you take negative feedback constructively than if you read such feedback as a sign that you weren't cut out for programming. MATLAB will not give you an error message that says

```
??? You don't deserve oxygen!
```

A more likely message is something prosaic like

```
??? Subscript indices must either be real positive
integers or logicals.
```

in response to code such as

```
Reaction_Time_For_Trial(0) = 680;
```

All one has to do in this situation is appreciate that it makes no sense to have the zero-th element of an array. An array can have a first element, a second element, a third element, and so on, but it can't have an element numbered zero. Whether the 0 was entered in the code due to a misunderstanding or a typo, you can correct the error without indicting your genes. Assuming you were describing the first trial, you could write

```
Reaction_Time_For_Trial(1) = 680;
```

It bears remembering that the error messages you'll receive while programming come from a machine, not from a person who knows what you are trying to say. When you receive an error message, it will help you to take the message as a piece of advice. Over time, you will get fewer error messages concerning low-level aspects of coding (e.g., when you have an unequal number of opening and closing parentheses in a line of code), and you will learn what the error messages mean. Interpreting error messages takes some practice because many of the messages are opaque relative to what you intend with your program. MATLAB error messages are more informative than the error messages in some other programming languages, but they do take some getting used to.

Over time you will also learn to court disaster when you program. I encourage you to do so. What I mean is that you should try to write programs that are resilient rather than brittle. If you write a program that crashes or yields crazy results when it gets input of a different sort than what you anticipated, your program won't be of much good. For example, if you write a program that is used to collect questionnaire data and a participant types in an age of –83, this could wreak havoc with subsequent data analyses. It doesn't matter why the participant put a minus sign in front of his or her age. Perhaps s/he thought this might help you see the number more clearly, perhaps it was just a typo, or perhaps s/he thought s/he was being cute. The point is that you must anticipate such eventualities. All sorts of things can go wrong when a program is being run. A good programmer guards against such eventualities. In this sense, being open to negative feedback means more than not letting your feelings be hurt when the computer beeps because you left out a punctuation mark or mistyped the name of a function. Being open to negative feedback also means being open to all sorts of unwanted events and building safeguards into your programs so you are not confronted with bogus results later on.

The final sense in which it is important to be open to negative results is that you should not be complacent when your program runs and gives you results, especially beautiful results, that cause you to blush with quixotic pride. An example follows.

The numbers 1 through 8 are assigned to a matrix called x. These numbers are session numbers, which comprise the independent variable of a fictional behavioral science study. The dependent variable is y, a set of fictional scores. After x and y have been defined, a command is used to plot the data. This command ends with a special instruction, in quotes, to plot the data in black (k), using circles (o), and using connecting lines (−). Within the plot command, we accidentally (or on purpose for this example) tell MATLAB to plot x along the horizontal axis and also along the vertical axis, rather than telling MATLAB to plot x along the horizontal axis and y along the vertical axis. Three more lines of code follow. One sets the limits of the x axis to ensure that the first point is plotted (a need that arises for this particular graph). The second specifies the label for the x axis, using the xlabel command. The third specifies the label for the y axis, using the ylabel command. (More details about these commands are given in Chapter 9. You can just skim over them here.)

Code 1.8.1

```
x = [1 2 3 4 5 6 7 8];
y = [0.39  0.47  0.60  0.21  0.57  0.36  0.64  0.32];
plot(x,x,'ko-')
xlim([.999 8])
xlabel('Session')
ylabel('Score on Test')
```

When we look at the output, we are impressed with the beauty of the results.

Output 1.8.1

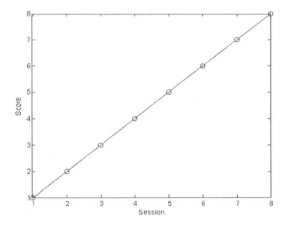

Before calling a press conference, it is advisable to check what happened. In this case, the results look too good to be true, and in fact they are. An error was made. When the error is found and fixed (with a comment inserted in the program accordingly), the results look quite different.

Code 1.8.2

```
x = [1 2 3 4 5 6 7 8];
y = [0.39  0.47  0.60  0.21  0.57  0.36  0.64  0.32];
plot(x,y,'ko-')  % Correction made here.
xlim([.999 8])
xlabel('Session')
ylabel('Score on Test')
```

Output 1.8.2

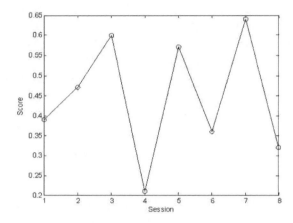

The point of this example is that you should avoid being too self-congratulatory. Be open to negative feedback, including negative feedback from yourself.

1.9   Programming With a Friend

No matter how open you may be to negative feedback, it is hard to catch all the mistakes you may make. And no matter how useful it may be to talk aloud in forming your plan for a computer program, you may feel uncomfortable speaking to no one in particular, especially when others are within earshot. (Pretending to be on your cell phone might help, but others could still get the wrong idea about you.)

A good way to avoid these problems is to have a friend by your side while you program. This is one of the best ways to program, at least in my opinion. Apart from the fact that the interactions can be fun, having two pairs of eyes and ears working on a problem can spur creativity. I encourage you to program with someone else. If you are using this book in a course, I also encourage your instructor to find ways of grading your work so cooperation with others counts for you and not against you.

1.10   Writing Concise Programs

It is fairly easy to write a program that has many unnecessary variables and superfluous lines. It is harder, at least early in training, to write a program that does the same job with few variables and lines. It becomes a source of pride to programmers when they write concise programs. Such programs do more than appeal to programmers' aesthetic sense. Concise programs also tend to finish in less time than programs that are verbose, run on and on, are redundant, and have far too many words in them, as is the case with this needlessly long sentence which should have ended long ago! Sometimes, but not always, a very concise program can reduce the time to run a program by seconds, minutes, hours, or even days. If the program must solve a problem on which people's lives depend, finding a quick solution can literally mean the difference between life and death.

1.11   Writing Clear Programs

Program conciseness should not be pursued at the expense of program clarity. Just as you should be as lucid as possible about what your program must do (Principle 2 in the previous list), you should write programs that are as easy to read and to understand as possible. Program clarity becomes especially important when you have written many programs. Returning to a program you wrote before and finding yourself unable to understand it can be very frustrating.

There are several things you can do to make your programs clear. One is to allow for extra lines of code or extra variables to make the structure of the program transparent. For example, if you need to divide one term by another and the numerator and denominator both contain complex expressions, it will probably help to have a variable for the terms in the numerator and another variable for the terms in the denominator. The division can then be expressed as the ratio of those two variables. The program might have a few more variables than are strictly required, but it will be easier for you and others to understand the code later on.

A second practice to make your code clear is to give your variables meaningful names. For example, in the program presented earlier (Code 1.7.1 and 1.7.2), it would have helped to call the independent variable `session` rather than `x` and to call the dependent variable `score` rather than `y`. Using those meaningful terms might have prevented the accidental plotting of `x` against `x` rather than the more appropriate plotting of `y` against `x`.

A third practice to improve program clarity is to add comments. Comments are non-executable statements. In MATLAB, comments are preceded by a percent sign (`%`), as in Code 1.7.2.

Programmers comment in different ways. Some intersperse comments with executable lines of code. Others tend to provide comments above the executable code at the start of the program and they then put relatively few comments in the body of the program. I prefer the latter method because it allows me to provide a conceptual plan for the program to follow, along with introductions of the variables I will be using. I prefer not to have too many comments interspersed with code within my programs because I find them distracting to read and (I confess) a pain to write.

Given that I like to provide comments at the start of my programs, I often begin my programming sessions by combining the need for commenting with the need for speaking aloud. Developing a plan for a program, as I said earlier in this Chapter(Section 1.5), is often aided by putting the plan into words. Being able to say what your program should do almost always helps you write the code you need. Therefore, in my own case, I often sit down and start typing the description of what my program will do, editing the emerging comment until I reach the point where I feel the procedure I'm describing is as clear and mechanically doable as I think I can make it. Then I begin coding, testing one part of the code at a time, saving successive edits in files with higher and higher version numbers.

Here is an example of one such program. The comments in the opening section (before any executable statements occur) are typical of what I write for myself. In a short program like this, no further comments are usually needed because once one gains familiarity with MATLAB, the meanings of the executable statements can usually be understood if the context is clear. All of the following commands are explained in greater detail later in the book.

Code 1.11.1

```
% Largest_So_Far_01
% Find the largest value in the one-row matrix d.
% Initialize largest_so_far to minus infinity.
% Then go through the matrix, by first setting i to 1
% and then letting i increase to the value equal
% to the number of elements of d, given by length(d).
% If the ith value of d is greater than largest_so_far,
% redefine largest_so_far as the ith value of d.
% After going through the whole array, print out
% largest_so_far.
d = [7 33 39 26 8 18 15 4 0];
largest_so_far = -inf;
for i = 1:length(d)
    if d(i) > largest_so_far
        largest_so_far = d(i);
    end
end
largest_so_far
```

Output 1.11.1

```
largest_so_far =
    39
```

The foregoing program can be adapted to find the largest value of other arrays, including much larger ones. I include the program here to give you a taste for what MATLAB programs look like. I also want to convey the idea that it is advisable to test programs on small scales. In general, it is advisable to work on toy problems before scaling up to larger ones. This program was tested with an array of length 9. This is a better length to start with than 1,000,000.

1.12   Understanding How the Chapters of This Book Are Organized

If you are persuaded that it makes sense for you to go further with this book, it will help you to understand how the book's chapters are organized. Each chapter begins with the sentence, "This chapter covers the following topics:" after which those subjects are listed. The way the subjects are listed is via presentation of the chapters' section names. All the section names of this book begin with gerunds, such as Understanding ..., Approaching ..., Deciding ... and so on. The sections are titled this way because I want you to learn by doing. You should be actively engaged in Understanding, Approaching, and Deciding (to name some activities) as you pursue the material presented here.

Continuing with the layout of the chapters, after all the section titles are given, every chapter continues with the sentence, "The commands that are introduced and the sections in which they are premiered are as follows." This sentence precedes a list of all the new commands introduced in the chapter along with the sections in which those new command are first discussed. If you run your finger down the list and find the activity to which it corresponds, you should be able to turn to that section and then find an example of how the command is used. Having examples of code can be one of the best ways to learn to program because you can edit the examples for your own needs.

Every program shown in this book has a code number. The first number (to the left of the decimal point) corresponds to the chapter in which the code appears. The second number (between the two decimal points) corresponds to the section in which the code appears. The third number (to the right of the second decimal point) is the number of the code within the section. The code itself appears in Courier font, as do all the terms in the main text body which are taken from the code.

Every program that yields output has its output shown in the same format as the code. The output is numbered.

One thing missing from the programs shown in this book are extensive comments. I have left them out not because comments are unimportant but because, for most of the programs in this book, the comments are presented in the text leading up to the programs. If you imagine percent signs in front of the lines of text preceding some code, you effectively have the kind of comment that can be supplied in a program itself.

1.13   Using the Website Associated With This Book

As you leaf through this book, you will see that all the graphs and images are in grayscale. The programs that yield these graphs and images allow for color graphics. The reason the book has grayscale images is to keep the cost of production down, which translates into a lower price for you. You can see the color images generated by the programs by going to the website associated with this book: www.matlab-behave.com. You will be able to copy the programs and outputs to use as you wish.

1.14   Acknowledging Limits

The final section of this chapter is concerned with the limits of this book, my limits as the book's author, and the limits of MATLAB itself. It is important for you to know what these limits are so you won't form unrealistic expectations.

First, you will not be able to program in MATLAB if you just read this book without also trying to program yourself. Reading how to program is a little like reading about riding a bike. You have to get on and try it yourself.

You should also know that the material presented in this book is meant to *acquaint* you with MATLAB but not to convey every aspect of this vast language and its associated applications. This book would be much denser if it went into many more detailed and advanced aspects of MATLAB. You should be able to delve into these topics on your own after having worked through the material presented here. In this connection, although there are a number of toolboxes associated with MATLAB (see Chapter 14), their contents are not discussed here. Instead, you should be able to use those toolboxes once you have learned the fundamentals of MATLAB conveyed in this book. Without knowing those fundamentals, it is unlikely that you will be able to make full use of the toolboxes.

A final comment about the limits of the book is that while the program examples presented here should be congenial to you as a behavioral scientist or as a student of behavioral science, not all of the program examples are centered on a particular behavioral approach or finding. Because the interests of behavioral scientists are highly varied, many of the examples offered here are generic rather than specific.

I must admit that I have never taken a computer science course and have never been systematically tutored by a professional programmer. I taught myself MATLAB and, before that, PASCAL, and before that, FORTRAN. I consider myself a pretty good programmer but I am not a true expert. Because my background is in psychology rather than computer science, mathematics, or engineering, I have used MATLAB for applications that are less technical than much of what MATLAB actually affords, and my use of the language has not fully exploited all that it permits, especially with regard to linear algebra or object-oriented programming. Be forewarned, then, that I have written this book to the best of my ability as a traditionally educated behavioral scientist, not as a technically trained computer scientist.

Third, you should know about the limits of MATLAB, at least in the incarnation used in the preparation of this book (R2006a, released March 1, 2006). The "word on the street" about MATLAB is that it is terrific for graphics and for creating conceptual models. Its reputation is less secure when it comes to real-time data gathering (EPrime is favored by many experimental psychologists for this purpose), and when it comes to number crunching that involves very large data sets, C/C++ or SAS may be better. On the other hand, MATLAB is being actively enhanced in so many quarters that its limitations, whatever they may be, will probably wane over time. Perhaps based on your introduction to MATLAB through this book, you will be one of the people who will improve MATLAB's capabilities or use MATLAB to make new discoveries in behavioral science or a kindred field.

2.   Interacting With MATLAB

This chapter covers the following topics:

2.1   Using MATLAB's windows
2.2   Using the `Command` window
2.3   Writing tiny programs in the `Command` window
2.4   Allowing or suppressing outputs by omitting or including end-of-line semicolons
2.5   Editing, saving, and running program scripts (`.m` files)
2.6   Running and debugging programs
2.7   Keeping a `diary`
2.8   Practicing interacting with MATLAB

The commands that are introduced and the sections in which they are premiered are as follows:

`calendar`	(2.2)
`clc`	(2.2)
`computer`	(2.2)
`ctrl—c`	(2.2)
`date`	(2.2)
`doc`	(2.2)
`edit`	(2.2)
`exit`	(2.2)
`help`	(2.2)
`license`	(2.2)
`ls`	(2.2)
`open`	(2.2)
`pwd`	(2.2)
`quit`	(2.2)
`up arrow`	(2.2)
`version`	(2.2)
`who`	(2.2)
`whos`	(2.2)
`;`	(2.4)
`%`	(2.5)
`...`	(2.5)
`commandwindow`	(2.5)
`ctrl—R`	(2.5)
`ctrl_T`	(2.5)
`F5`	(2.5)
`Run`	(2.5)
`diary`	(2.6)

2.1   Using MATLAB's Windows

To use MATLAB, you have to activate it and access its range of functions. MATLAB is activated, as most computer applications are, by clicking on its icon on the computer desktop or wherever its icon is located.

After MATLAB is activated, the **Command Window** appears. This is the most important window in MATLAB because it is where you control what happens and where you see the results of your programming efforts. The **Command Window** will be described in more detail in Section 2.2.

Another important window is the **Edit** window. Here you invoke MATLAB's editing capabilities by writing, revising, and saving program scripts (files that end with a `.m` suffix). The **Editor** will be discussed in Section 2.3.

Other windows are used on a more optional basis. These windows, like the **Command Window** and **Editor** window, are accessible at the top of the MATLAB screen via the **Windows** tab or **Desktop** tab.

One of these optional windows is the **Help** window, which provides a portal to MATLAB's vast, and sometimes labyrinthine, tutorials.

Another is the **Command History** window, which chronicles the commands you have used.

The **Current Directory** window lists the contents of the current directory for MATLAB. You will learn how to change the **Current Directory** in Chapter 6 (**Input–Output**). By default, the **Current Directory** is called **Work**.

The **Workspace** window lists the variables that are currently active, giving their names, values, and class. The values of a variable can be viewed in spreadsheet form by clicking on the grid icon to the left of its name.

Other windows, called **Figure** windows, can be created, opened, and closed in your programs. Details are given in Chapter 8 (**Plots**).

2.2   Using the Command Window

As mentioned previously, after MATLAB is activated, it brings up the Command Window. This is the window where you can issue commands. Commands for MATLAB can be typed following the >> prompt. Some useful commands that can be typed in after the >> prompt are given below, followed by the functions they serve. It will be helpful for you to read through the list at this stage because the commands are listed more or less chronologically, in a way that corresponds to what might occur in a typical MATLAB session. Some of the commands tend to be used more than others. The most frequent ones, in my experience, are `help`, `ls`, `open`, `ctrl—c`, and `exit`.

`license`	The license for the MATLAB application being used. This can be important when soliciting help from Mathworks.
`version`	The version number of MATLAB program being used, also important for soliciting help from Mathworks.

`computer`	The kind of computer being used.
`date`	The current date.
`calendar`	The calendar for the current month.
`help`	Topics for which help can be provided within the command window. Adding a topic name after `help` (followed by a space) brings up help about that topic, provided it is known to MATLAB. You can find out what topics are known to MATLAB by first typing `help` alone. This brings up all the categories for which `help` is available.
`doc`	This is a shortcut to the Help navigator, where all the help that can be viewed in the Command window is available, plus much more. The Help navigator can also be accessed via the Help tab at the top of the MATLAB screen.
`pwd`	Lists the current directory, which by default is the MATLAB Work folder.
`ls`	Lists the contents of the current directory. Adding just part of a file name after `ls` (following a space) with an asterisk before or after the given part of the file name causes all the files with that named part to be listed. Thus, `ls tim*` lists `tim_program_01.m`, `tim_program_02.m`, `timmy_program_101.m`, and `timothy.doc` if these files exist in the current directory. `ls t*.m` lists `tim_program_02.m`, `timmy_program_101.m`, but not `timothy.doc`.
`edit`	Creates a file or opens an existing file in MATLAB's own editor. If the name of a file is put in after `edit` (following a space), that file is opened for editing, provided it is in the current directory.
`open`	Opens a file in the current directory or invokes other programs as needed (e.g., Adobe Acrobat for .pdf files).
`who`	Lists the names of the currently active variables
`whos`	Lists the names of the currently active variables as well as their sizes (i.e., the number of rows and columns in each of their matrices), how much memory they use, and the type of variable they are. The amount of memory is given in bytes. A byte is a string of 8 bits. A bit is a binary digit equal to 1 or 0.
`ctrl–c`	Holding the ctrl key and the c key at the same time on a PC or the apple key and the c key at the same time on a Mac interrupts the program currently being run. This is very useful when you have runaway programs for

	which unwanted data are being spewed on the screen or when you have a program that's running for a long time without any output.
up arrow	Hitting the up arrow on the keyboard after the >> prompt *n* times brings you back *n* command lines. Thus, hitting the up arrow once brings you back to the last command.
clc	Clears the command window
exit	Terminates MATLAB
quit	Terminates MATLAB, but only after completing a program called FINISH.m whose contents can be altered by the user.

2.3   Writing Tiny Programs in the Command Window

The foregoing list of commands is just a small fraction of the commands that can potentially be typed in the command window. In fact, the number of possible commands that can be typed in the command window is infinite, because entire series of commands can be typed or pasted after the command line prompt (>>). In practice, typing or pasting very long series of commands is not a good idea. it is much better to generate program scripts offline in MATLAB's editor, where the scripts can be saved and subsequently modified. We will turn to the editor in the next section. In this section, we consider tiny programs that can be written in the command window (or created and stored with the editor before being run). We consider these tiny programs here because experienced MATLAB users often type simple commands, such as the ones previously mentioned, into the command window. Furthermore, the rules governing acceptable command syntax hold regardless of whether the commands are added to the command line by hand or through the editor.

One of the most fundamental programming tasks is to assign a value to a variable. Suppose you want to assign the number 2 to some variable, arbitrarily called A. This can be done by typing A = 2 after the command line prompt as follows:

Code 2.3.1:

```
A = 2
```

Output 2.3.1:

```
A =
     2
```

The ordering of terms in the assignment is important, as follows.

Code 2.3.2:

```
2 = A
```

Output 2.3.2:

```
??? 2 = A

Error: The expression to the left of the equals sign is
not a valid target for an assignment.
```

The error message indicates that order matters in MATLAB. This contrasts with the rules of mathematics, where both sides of an equation mean the same thing regardless of whether terms appear to the left or right of the equal sign. Thus, in MATLAB, `2 = A` does not mean the same thing as `A = 2`. Programmers often say "A gets 2" when referring to statements such as `A = 2` to indicate that they are referring to a variable assignment rather than to a conventional mathematical equation.

In MATLAB, variable names, program names and other file names are case sensitive. Thus, if you query MATLAB about the value of `A`, you can get a satisfying, if not terribly exciting, result:

Code 2.3.3:

```
A
```

Output 2.3.3:

```
A =
    2
```

If you ask MATLAB about the value of a variable called `a`, which you innocently believe is the same as `A`, you get an error message:

Code 2.3.4:

```
a
```

Output 2.3.4:

```
??? Undefined function or variable 'a'.
```

it is not that MATLAB cannot tolerate lower-case variable names, for it is fine to assign a value to `a`:

Code 2.3.5:

```
a = 3
```

Output 2.3.5:

```
a =
    3
```

You can even begin to carry out some computations using your two variables, a and A, assigning a new variable to the result:

Code 2.3.6:

```
My_Difference = a — A
```

Output 2.3.6:

```
My_Difference =
      1
```

The last example shows that the name of a variable need not be restricted to a single letter. It can be a string such as `My_Difference`. Spaces are not permitted in variable names or in names of programs or other files. However, spaces are important for meaningful phrases like My Difference. A substitute for a space is a subscript line or some other device (e.g., upper-case letters to signify new words within strings of lowercase letters). Be aware that variable names cannot start with numbers. They also cannot include special characters ($, %, &, @, −, +, *, /, \, ^, or ,). Finally, variable names cannot be reserved words for MATLAB (e.g., `if`, `for`, and `end`). You will encounter these reserved words later in this book, and you needn't worry about remembering them at this stage, because if you assign a variable to a reserved word in MATLAB, you will get an error message:

Code 2.3.7:

```
for = 4
```

Output 2.3.7:

```
??? for = 4;

Error: The expression to the left of the equals sign is
not a valid target for an assignment.
```

This is one example where relying on error messages is a help rather than a hindrance. One nice thing about error messages is that you can click on them and you will be brought back to the line of code that caused the error message to appear.

Must a variable name be supplied for the result of every new computation? The answer is No, as seen in Code 2.3.8. Here, where no output variable is declared, MATLAB automatically assigns the output to a variable called `ans`, which, presumably, is short for answer.

Code 2.3.8:

```
a + A
```

Output 2.3.8:

```
ans =
     5
```

You can inquire into the value of `ans` just as you can inquire into the value of any other variable:

Code 2.3.9:

```
ans
```

Output 2.3.9:

```
ans =
     5
```

2.4   Allowing or Suppressing Outputs by Omitting or Including End-of-Line Semicolons

Omitting or including a semicolon at the end of a line of code has an important effect. Omitting the semicolon permits screen output. Including the semicolon stops screen output.

For example, if you type `My_Difference` followed by a semicolon, the result is initially disappointing.

Code 2.4.1:

```
My_Difference;
```

Output 2.4.1:

```
>>
```

Apparently, nothing happened. In a sense this is true because `My_Difference` already had a value assigned to it.

If you do a new computation and follow it with a semicolon, you again seem to get the same null effect:

Code 2.4.2:

```
My_Difference_2 = A − My_Difference;
```

Output 2.4.2:

```
>>
```

However, the computation has been carried out, as you can confirm by typing `My_Dif-ference_2` without a semicolon at the end:

Code 2.4.3:

```
My_Difference_2
```

Output 2.4.3:

```
My_Difference_2 =
     1
```

Suppressing outputs by adding a semicolon at the end of a command can be very useful. Omitting a semicolon and having a large matrix printed in the command window can be disconcerting. You can break out of the salvo of unwanted output by interrupting the program with `ctrl-c`. However, it is better to get into the habit of adding semicolons to the ends of lines, removing them in those special circumstances when you want to see the results of particular lines. The practice of including and omitting semicolons at the ends of lines of code in MATLAB is so important that I have devoted an entire section to this one feature of the language.

2.5   Editing, Saving, and Running MATLAB Programs

As already mentioned, it makes more sense to compose and save program scripts offline, using MATLAB's editor, than to type or paste commands into the command window. Composing program scripts offline lets you work on them incrementally. You can add to them a little at a time after checking that the components work as expected. Saving the scripts lets you use them later.

The accepted procedure for invoking the editor when you want to create a new program is to click at the top left corner of the MATLAB screen on the small white rectangle with the folded corner. This brings up a blank screen in the editor.

I recommend that you next write the name of the program as a comment. A comment is a non-executable string, marked by a percent sign (%) to its left at the start of each line. I usually write the title of a program as a comment, then I immediately select and copy the title alone (i.e., without the % sign), and go to Save As, pasting the name of the program into the Save As window. Here is an example of a small program with comments:

Code 2.5.1:

```
% My_Program_01
% A program to add two numbers called X and Y.
X = 10;
Y = 12;
Z = X + Y
% end of program
```

Output 2.5.1:

```
Z =
    22
```

To get the output, I pasted the name of the program into the Save As window, hit return, and was gratified to see that the script was saved as a MATLAB script, so defined by its `.m` suffix. To run the program, I clicked on the Run icon (the rectangle with horizontal lines and a downward pointing arrow to its left). There are other ways to run a program from the edit window. One way is to click on Debug and then click on Run. Another way, in Windows, is to hit the F5 key. You can also run a program directly from the command window by typing or pasting its name (without the `.m` suffix) into the command line and then hitting Return or Enter.

One inconvenience in getting the output in this example was that I had to manually switch to the command window to see what Z turned out to be (not that the suspense was all that great). There is a way to automatically activate the command window. That is to include `commandwindow` in your program.

There are a couple of other points that are worth keeping in mind in connection with using the editor to write MATLAB scripts. One is that each command must begin on a new line. If the command is long enough to stretch beyond one visible line on the computer screen, you can add an ellipsis (...) at the end of the line and continue the command on the next line. Here is an example.

Code 2.5.2:

```
% Ellipsis_Illustration
Method_1_Score_1 = 899;
Method_2_Score_1 = 1286;
Method_1_Score_2 = 1018;
Method_2_Score_2 = 1344;
Method_1_Score_3 = 1167;
Method_2_Score_3 = 1389;

Summed_Differences_Between_Method_2_and_Method_1_Scores = ...
     Method_2_Score_1 — Method_1_Score_1 + ...
     Method_2_Score_2 — Method_1_Score_2 + ...
     Method_2_Score_3 — Method_1_Score_3
```

Output 2.5.2:

```
Summed_Differences_Between_Method_2_and_Method_1_Scores =
    935
```

A second point to bear in mind is that the editor provides convenient tools for indenting and outdenting lines of code. This is especially useful when creating `for` loops, `if—then` loops, and `while` loops, which will be discussed in Chapter 5. The key combinations that allow for indenting and outdenting of commands are accessible under the Text bar of the

MATLAB edit window and can be easily learned. Also available under the Text bar are key combinations that let you turn executable code into a comment (ctrl–R in Windows or Apple–R on the Mac) and for turning a comment into executable code (ctrl–T in Windows or Apple–R on the Mac).

A final remark about editing, saving, and running MATLAB programs is that you cannot run a program if MATLAB's editor is on but MATLAB itself is not on. MATLAB's editor can be activated without activating MATLAB. So be careful not to open a script and try to run it when MATLAB is off. The program will not run in that circumstance. Get in the habit of activating MATLAB and then opening files for editing afterward.

2.6   Running and Debugging MATLAB Programs

Perhaps the most challenging aspect of programming is making sure that your program does what you want. it is easy to tell that your program *isn't* doing what you want when your program won't run at all—that is, when the MATLAB compiler gives an error message. Correcting a program that either will not run or yields odd results is known as *debugging*. Debugging is one of the most important activities in programming. Ideally, debugging should never be necessary. Ideally, each of us should be so clear-headed and so accurate in our input of code that we never make mistakes. Alas, the real world is different, and debugging is an important activity that all programmers must endure.

How should you debug your programs? Different people take different approaches. Some people take advantage of MATLAB's debugging resources. You can learn about these by using MATLAB's help options (e.g., typing `help debug` in the command window). Others prefer a more homespun approach of developing very small programs or parts of programs, testing them under a variety of conditions, and then, once they are satisfied that the programs work correctly, adding a little more to the program and repeating the quality check. This is the method I use and strongly endorse.

One piece of advice I can offer in connection with this incremental approach to programming is to follow the adage, "If it ain't broke, don't fix it." Once you have a program that works, before modifying it to do something else, save the working program using a new name and make sure that the old, previously saved program is still available. Thus, if `Behavior_22.m` works well, save a new version called `Behavior_23.m` before you start making any changes. Remember that computer storage is cheap. Your time is not.

2.7   Keeping a Diary

You can keep a record of the text that appeared in the command window of a MATLAB session by using the `diary` function. When MATLAB is activated, `diary` is off. However, you can activate `diary` with the `diary on` command or you can simply type `diary`, which toggles the state of `diary` from off to on. You can also designate the file to which you want the diary to be saved with a command such as `diary('my_diary')`. This command only works after you have activated `diary`. You can subsequently turn `diary` off with the `diary off` command or by simply typing `diary`, which toggles the state of `diary` from on to off.

2.8   Practicing Interacting With MATLAB

Try your hand at the following exercises, using only the methods introduced so far in this book or information given in the problems themselves.

Problem 2.8.1

Open MATLAB's command window and get today's date.

Problem 2.8.2

In MATLAB's command window, get this month's calendar.

Problem 2.8.3

Next, look at this month's calendar from a year ago. Hint: Although nothing you have read in this chapter tells you directly how to do this, there is a mention of it in `help`.

Problem 2.8.4

Find out what time it is using MATLAB by getting help about `clock`. If you use the command `format bank`, the output will be more readable.

Problem 2.8.5

In the command window, add 2 + 2 and then request the value of `ans`.

Problem 2.8.6

In the command window, get the result of adding 4 to `ans`. Looking at the new answer, what does this tell you about MATLAB's "willingness" to redefine values?

Problem 2.8.7

Use the editor to write and then save a short program called `My_Program_01` which assigns 1 to `w`. Run the program so the value of `w` displays in the command window.

Problem 2.8.8

Save `My_Program_01` as `My_Program_02` and expand it so that after `w` gets 1, `x` gets `w` + 1, and then `y` gets `x` – 2. Add another one-line command that immediately brings up the command window.

Problem 2.8.9

Debug `My_Program_03` so `b` gets the sum of `a` and 3, `c` gets `b` – 2, `d` gets the product of `b` and `c`, and `e` gets `b` divided by `c`. Hint: Although you haven't been told that the signs are for multiplication or division, you can use `help +` to find out. The plus sign is used because it is the familiar addition operator.

```
% My_Program_03
ab = a + 1
c = = b — 2
d b × c
e = b divided by c
```

Problem 2.8.10

Write a program called My_Program_04 in which Code 2.5.1 is expanded so there is a Method_1_Score_4 which gets 1267 and a Method_2_Score_4 which gets 1289 and all scores used in method 1 and 2 are subtracted in the manner already established.

Problem 2.8.11

Doing these exercises has created a number of variables. Find out which variable uses the most computer storage. Hint: A good detective knows whos s/he is dealing with.

3. Matrices

This chapter covers the following topics:

The commands that are introduced and the sections in which they are premiered are as follows:

`end`	(3.2)
`length`	(3.4)
`size`	(3.4)
`'`	(3.5)
`linspace`	(3.6)
`logspace`	(3.6)
`who`	(3.7)
`whos`	(3.7)
`[ ]`	(3.8)
`clear`	(3.8)
`clear all`	(3.8)

3.1 Creating Matrices

One of the main reasons for using MATLAB is to deal with large data sets. Any such data set, if it is formatted in a way that MATLAB allows, can be stored and dealt with as a single variable. Saying this another way, a single variable, such as the ones defined in the last chapter, need not be assigned a single number. Instead, they can be assigned matrices with multiple elements. Here is an example of the assignment of a multi-element matrix of numbers to a variable called A.

Code 3.1.1:

```
A = [1, 2, 3, 4, 5, 6]
```

Output 3.1.1:

```
A =
     1    2    3    4    5    6
```

A matrix need not be restricted to integers. Recall that integers are "whole" numbers, or numbers which, in our decimal system, can be fully identified without adding any value to the right of the decimal point. Real numbers of any sort can represented in MATLAB matrices.

Code 3.1.2:

```
B = [4, .8, −.12, 0, −24]
```

Output 3.1.2:

```
B =
     4.0000   0.8000   −0.1200 0   −24.0000
```

In both of the preceding examples, commas sat between the numbers in the matrix. Commas are not necessary. Spaces will do, and matrices are usually written without commas, as in this example.

Code 3.1.3:

```
C = [4 .8 −.12 0 −24]
```

Output 3.1.3:

```
C =
     4.0000   0.8000   −0.1200 0   −24.0000
```

C is a 1×6 matrix. The number 1 refers to the number of *rows* in the matrix and the number 6 refers to the number of *columns*. A convention used in MATLAB, as in matrix algebra, is that the number of rows in a matrix is reported before the number of columns. For this reason, we often refer to a matrix of size $r \times c$. A way to remember this is to think of Royal-Crown, or RC® Cola. Because images are memorable, especially when they are bizarre or incongruous within the context in which they are presented, I include a picture of an RC Cola drink, intending this as a jog for memory, not as an endorsement of the product.

Figure 3.1.1

How can we define a matrix that has more than $r = 1$ row? Here we define a 3×2 matrix.

Code 3.1.4:

```
D = [1 2; 3 4; 5 6]
```

Output 3.1.4:

```
D =
     1    2
     3    4
     5    6
```

Inspection of the code used to define D shows how the 3×2 layout is achieved. A semicolon (;) indicates row endings. Thus, the semicolon has an important function in MATLAB besides suppressing print-outs (see Section 2.4). Semicolons within brackets indicate matrix row breaks. You can still use a semicolon at the end of an assignment to suppress printout, as in this example.

Code 3.1.5:

```
D = [1 2; 3 4; 5 6];
```

Output 3.1.5:

```
>>
```

MATLAB is very particular about the layout of matrices.

Code 3.1.6:

```
E = [1 2 3; 4 5; 6 7 8];
```

Output 3.1.6:

```
??? Error using ==> vertcat
All rows in the bracketed expression must have the same
number of columns.
```

As the error message reminds us, a matrix must have the same number of columns in each row. In Code 3.1.6, E was assigned a row of three columns followed by a row of two columns. This was problematic.

3.2 Locating Elements of Matrices

Having defined a correctly formatted matrix of numbers, you may want to access values occupying particular locations within that matrix. Suppose you want to know what the number is in row 1, column 1 of D. You can find out as follows, making sure there is no semicolon at the end of the statement so you can see the output you want.

Code 3.2.1:

```
D(1,1)
```

Output 3.2.1:

```
ans =
      1
```

Similarly, if you want to know what number occupies row 2, column 2 of D, you can use the following.

Code 3.2.2:

```
D(2,2)
```

Output 3.2.2:

```
ans =
      4
```

Suppose you want to know all the values in column 1 over all of the rows of D. You can put a colon (:) in the row position and a 1 in the column position:

Code 3.2.2:

```
D(:,1)
```

Output 3.2.2:

```
ans =
      1
      3
      5
```

Similarly, if you want to know all the values in column 2 over all the rows of D, you can put a colon in the row position and a 2 in the column position:

Code 3.2.3:

```
D(:,2)
```

Output 3.2.3:

```
ans =
      2
      4
      6
```

To find all the values in row 1 over all of D's columns, you can put a 1 in the row position and a colon in the column position:

Code 3.2.4:

```
D(1,:)
```

Output 3.2.4:

```
ans =
     1    2
```

These examples show that when a colon is inserted at a row or column position, it specifies all the values for that row or column. For this reason, the command D(: , :) is equivalent to the command D.

Just as the colon (:) is useful for locating elements of matrices in MATLAB, so too is the word end. To see how useful this term is, construct a matrix E.

Code 3.2.5:

```
E = [1  2  3  4;  5  6  7  8;  9  10  11  12]
```

Output 3.2.5:

```
E =
     1    2    3    4
     5    6    7    8
     9   10   11   12
```

To get the element in the last row, second column, you can write the following.

Code 3.2.6:

```
E(end,2)
```

Output 3.2.6:

```
ans =
    10
```

To get the second row, last column, you can write

Code 3.2.7:

```
E(2,end)
```

Output 3.2.7:

```
ans =
     8
```

To get the second-to-the-last value in the second row, you can write

Code 3.2.8:

```
E(2,end-1)
```

Output 3.2.8:

```
ans =
      7
```

3.3   Concatenating Matrices

Matrices can be joined together or, to use the more technical term, concatenated. You can concatenate the matrices F and G into matrix H as follows.

Code 3.3.1:

```
F = [10 11 12];
G = [13 14 15];
H = [F;G]
```

Output 3.3.1:

```
H =
    10   11   12
    13   14   15
```

Notice that the semicolon in the assignment to H has the same effect as it did when placed inside brackets. It inserts a return. If we omit the semicolon and replace it with a space or a comma, the result, in this case, is a one-row matrix.

Code 3.3.2:

```
H = [F G]
```

Output 3.3.2:

```
H =
    10   11   12   13   14   15
```

Concatenating two matrices with different numbers of rows and columns is not allowed.

```
I = [20 21 22 23 24 25 26];
```

Code 3.3.3:

```
J = [H;I]
```

Output 3.3.3:

```
??? Error using ==> vertcat
All rows in the bracketed expression must have the same
number of columns.
```

On the other hand, even though H and I have different numbers of columns, there is no problem with concatenating these two matrices in a new matrix that has just one row:

Code 3.3.4:

```
K = [H I]
```

Output 3.3.4:

```
K =
    10   11   12   13   14   15   20   21   22   23   24   25   26
```

3.4   Determining the Size of a Matrix

Before concatenating large matrices, it is useful to check the size of each one. The size of a matrix, as mentioned earlier in this chapter, is its number of rows and columns. So the size of matrix I is [1, 7]. The first value is the number of rows. The second value is the number of columns. You can find the size of a matrix with the `size` function. (Functions are treated in detail in Chapter 8.)

Code 3.4.1:

```
size(I)
```

Output 3.4.1:

```
ans =
     1    7
```

The size of matrix K can be found in the same way, and the resulting array can be assigned to a matrix called, in this instance, `sz_K`.

Code 3.4.2:

```
sz_K = size(K)
```

Output 3.4.2:

```
sz_K =
     1   17
```

The number of rows and number of columns that are identified by the `size` function can be assigned directly to two elements of a new matrix whose elements can be called `rows` and `columns`:

Code 3.4.3:

```
[rows columns] = size(K)
```

Output 3.4.3:

```
rows =
     1

columns =
      17
```

For a matrix with just one row, the `length` of the matrix is the number of elements in that row. Similarly, for a matrix with just one column, the `length` of the matrix is the number of elements in that column. More generally, the `length` of a matrix equals the larger of its number of rows and columns. Studying the following lines of code can give you a feeling for `size` and `length`.

Code 3.4.4:

```
JJ = [1:4;5:8]
```

Output 3.4.4:

```
JJ =
     1    2    3    4
     5    6    7    8
```

Code 3.4.5:

```
size(JJ)
```

Output 3.4.5:

```
ans =
     2    4
```

Code 3.4.6:

```
length(JJ)
```

Output 3.4.6:

```
ans =
     4
```

Code 3.4.7:

```
KK = [1 5; 2 6; 3 7; 4 8]
```

Output 3.4.7:

```
ans =
     1    5
     2    6
     3    7
     4    8
```

Code 3.4.8:

```
length(KK)
```

Output 3.4.8:

```
ans =
     4
```

When you have a matrix with more than one row or column, I suggest using `size` rather than `length` to avoid confusion.

3.5   Transposing a Matrix

Suppose you have two matrices, J and K, defined as follows.

Code 3.5.1:

```
J = [1 2 3 4];
K = [5;6;7;8]
```

Output 3.5.1:

```
K =
     5
     6
     7
     8
```

Because there are no semicolons between the values in K, J is of size [1, 4]. On the other hand, because there *are* semicolons between the values in K, K is of size [4, 1]. If you try to concatenate J and K, you get an error message.

Code 3.5.2:

```
L = [J;K]
```

Output 3.5.2:

```
??? Error using ==> vertcat
All rows in the bracketed expression must have the same
number of columns.
```

You can get around this problem if necessary by "turning one matrix around." More technically, you can *transpose* the matrix so its rows and columns are interchanged. MATLAB lets you transpose a matrix simply by adding an apostrophe (').

Code 3.5.3:

```
K'
```

Output 3.5.3:

```
ans =
     5   6   7   8
```

Matrices J and K' can now be concatenated into a two-row matrix:

Code 3.5.4:

```
L = [J;K']
```

Output 3.5.4:

```
L =
     1   2   3   4
     5   6   7   8
```

If you wish to take the transpose of L, you can do so easily:

Code 3.5.4:

```
L'
```

Output 3.5.4:

```
ans =
     1   5
     2   6
     3   7
     4   8
```

As seen here, the first row becomes the first column and the second row becomes the second column.

3.6   Creating Matrices With Shorthand Methods

All the matrices we have considered so far are very small. If you need to create a very large matrix, it is clearly tedious to type in all the values by hand. Fortunately, MATLAB provides short-hand methods for creating matrices. These short-hand methods are also convenient for accessing values within matrices.

Consider the matrix `M`:

Code 3.6.1:

```
M = [1 2 3 4 5 6];
```

An easier way to create this matrix is as follows:

Code 3.6.2:

```
M = [1:6]
```

Output 3.6.2:

```
M =
     1   2   3   4   5   6
```

The colon tells MATLAB that you want a range of values, in this case from 1 to 6.

MATLAB lets you specify the increments for the range of values you want. Suppose you want values from 1 to 6, increasing in steps of .5. This can be achieved, as shown here for a matrix arbitrarily called `MM`.

Code 3.6.3:

```
MM = [1:.5:6]
```

Output 3.6.3:

```
MM =
       1.0000   1.5000   2.0000   2.5000   3.0000   3.5000
   4.0000   4.5000   5.0000   5.5000   6.0000
```

You can look at these values in a more readable format by transposing the matrix.

Code 3.6.4:

```
MM'
```

Output 3.6.4:

```
ans =
          1.0000
          1.5000
          2.0000
          2.5000
          3.0000
          3.5000
          4.0000
          4.5000
          5.0000
          5.5000
          6.0000
```

This example shows that inserting a value followed by a colon between the starting and ending values of a matrix (in this case, `.5:`) lets you specify the size of the steps to be taken from the starting value to the ending value.

Earlier, when we typed `M = [1:6]`, MATLAB "knew" that the step size was 1. Why was that the case? The value of 1 was *implicit*. When no value is given in a matrix definition, MATLAB assumes that the desired step size is 1. The notion that some values are implicit is a very important one. Often, when using MATLAB, you can find sources of flexibility by considering whether there might be a way of specifying a value that seems to be assumed by MATLAB. Specific examples will come up later—for example, when you learn about properties of figures and the axes used in graphs.

Must all matrices have ascending values? Is there a short-hand way of creating matrices that have descending values? Not surprisingly, there is.

Code 3.6.5:

```
Descending_Matrix = [5: −2: −7]
```

Output 3.6.5:

```
Descending_Matrix =
      5    3    1   −1   −3   −5   −7
```

As this example shows, a negative step sign, coupled with an ending value that is smaller than the starting value, ensures a matrix with descending values.

Be sure that the ending value is the one you want.

Code 3.6.6:

```
s = [5: −6: −3]
```

Output 3.6.6:

```
s =
    5   −1
```

The final desired value of –3 does not appear here because you can't get to –3 from 5 in steps of –6.

Errors like this one can arise when you want to create a vector (a matrix with a single row or a single column) with a desired number of values, as for example, when you want to generate a graph with a desired number of points (see Chapter 8). There is a short-hand way to create such a matrix . You can use the `linspace` function.

Code 3.6.7:

```
s = linspace(5,−3,10);
s'
```

Output 3.6.7:

```
ans =
  5.0000
  4.1111
  3.2222
  2.3333
  1.4444
  0.5556
 −0.3333
 −1.2222
 −2.1111
 −3.0000
```

The `linspace` command, as used here, indicates that you want `s` to be a vector that runs from 5 to –3 with 10 values in all. As seen above, MATLAB has found a step size that yields the desired vector. The step size is the same throughout the matrix, which explains why `linspace` has the name it does. Elements are linearly spaced when the steps between them are the same.

Another function for generating vectors is `logspace`. As its name implies, `logspace` creates a vector whose elements are spaced logarithmically rather than linearly. To learn what `logspace` does (or to remind yourself at some later time), you can use `help` at the current line of the command window, just as you can use `help` to learn about other commands:

Code 3.6.8:

```
help logspace
```

Output 3.6.8:

```
LOGSPACE Logarithmically spaced vector.
  LOGSPACE(X1, X2) generates a row vector of 50
  logarithmically equally spaced points between decades
  10^X1 and 10^X2.
  If 2 is pi, then the points are     between 10^X1 and pi.

  LOGSPACE(X1, X2, N) generates N points.
  For N < 2, LOGSPACE returns 10^X2.

  See also LINSPACE, :.
```

What this is saying is that `logspace` generates N points equal to 10 raised to the X1 power up to 10 raised to the X2 power. When N is not specified, MATLAB sets N to 50.

To make sure you understand this, you can generate code to check that MATLAB creates a matrix `sss` that has five values spanning 10^1 to 10^2.

Code 3.6.9:

```
sss = logspace(1,2,5)
```

Output 3.6.9:

```
sss =
      10.0000 17.7828 31.6228 56.2341 100.0000
```

3.7 Checking the Status of Matrices

A number of matrices have been created in the programs listed in this chapter. What is the status of the matrices? It is useful to check which matrices are active, and this can be done either by activating the Workspace window (see Chapter 2) or by typing who in the command window. Here is the result of typing who after creating the matrices described above (and no others):

Code 3.7.1:

```
who
```

Output 3.7.1:

```
Your variables are:
Descending_Matrix      JJ        lg        sss
II                     ans       s
```

Typing whos rather than who gives more information about the currently active values:

Code 3.7.2:

```
whos
```

Output 3.7.2:

```
        Name                Size     Bytes   Class
        Descending_Matrix   1x7      56      double array
        II                  2x4      64      double array
        JJ                  4x2      64      double array
        Ans                 1x2      16      double array
        Lg                  1x5      40      double array
        S                   1x10     80      double array
        Sss                 1x5      40      double array
   Grand total is 45 elements using 360 bytes
```

As seen above, whos gives the name, size, number of bytes, and class of each active matrix. The term double array means an array of double-precision numbers, that is, 14 decimal digits for a number expressed in scientific notation. More information about data types is given in Chapter 7.

3.8 Clearing and Emptying Matrices

To remove a matrix, you can clear it. Suppose you wish to clear s.

Code 3.8.1:

```
clear s
whos
```

Output 3.8.1:

```
        Name                Size     Bytes   Class
        Descending_Matrix   1x7      56      double array
        II                  2x4      64      double array
        JJ                  4x2      64      double array
        Ans                 1x2      16      double array
        Lg                  1x5      40      double array
        Sss                 1x5      40      double array
   Grand total is 35 elements using 280 bytes
```

Comparing Output 3.8.1 to Output 3.7.2 shows that s is now gone.

You can clear all active variables by writing clear all. It is good to get into the habit of writing clear all at or near the start of a program when you want to work with a fresh slate.

To reduce the size of a matrix, you can empty some or all of its cells. The following example shows how you can remind yourself of the contents and size of a matrix—in this case sss—and then empty its last and next-to-last elements by assigning the null element [ ] to them.

Code 3.8.2:

```
sss
size(sss)
sss(end-1:end) = [ ]
size(sss)
```

Output 3.8.2:

```
sss =
      10.0000 17.7828 31.6228 56.2341 100.0000

      ans =
         1    5

ans =
      10.0000 17.7828 31.6228

ans =
       1    3
```

You can also empty sss entirely and check its new size.

Code 3.8.3:

```
sss = [ ]
size(sss)
```

Output 3.8.3:

```
sss =
      [ ]
ans =
      0    0
```

Emptying a matrix is not the same as clearing it. Clearing a matrix purges it entirely. After a matrix is emptied by setting it to [ ], the matrix is active and can be added to in subsequent steps. Indeed, an effective way of defining a new matrix to which values will be added is to set it initially to [ ], as in the first line of Code 3.8.3, above, and then to add elements to it, as in this example below.

Code 3.8.4:

```
matrix_to_be_added_to = [  ]
matrix_to_be_added_to =[matrix_to_be_added_to;  1]
matrix_to_be_added_to =[matrix_to_be_added_to;  2]
matrix_to_be_added_to =[matrix_to_be_added_to;  3]
matrix_to_be_added_to =[matrix_to_be_added_to;  4]
```

Output 3.8.4:

```
matrix_to_be_added_to =

    [  ]

matrix_to_be_added_to =

      1

matrix_to_be_added_to =

      1
      2

matrix_to_be_added_to =

      1
      2
      3

matrix_to_be_added_to =

      1
      2
      3
      4
```

To help convey the spirit of the foregoing code, what just happened is a little like adding one item after another to an empty pickup truck. Such a truck, affectionately referred to by its owner as `matrix_to_be_added_to`, is shown here as an aid for future memory.

Figure 3.8.1

3.9 Practicing With Matrices

Try your hand at the following exercises, using only the methods introduced so far in this book or information given in the problems themselves.

Problem 3.9.1

Create a matrix called A that increases in steps of 1 from 1 up to 1000

Problem 3.9.2

Create a matrix called B that decreases in steps of 3 from 333 down to 3

Problem 3.9.3

Create a matrix called C using bracket notation, and define C so [linspace (1,100,100) − C] is a row of 100 zero's.

Problem 3.9.4

Create a matrix called Even that has the first 200 positive even integers and another matrix called Odd that has the first 200 positive odd integers. Check the size of Even and the size of Odd to make sure the values are correct.

Problem 3.9.5

Repair the following matrix assignments:

D should run from 5 up to 100 in steps of .5

```
D = [5:-.5:100]
```

E should run from 5 down to −100 in steps of −.25

```
E = [5,25:100]
```

F should have 20 values from 1 to 10 that are logarithmically spaced

```
F, = linspace(−1,10.3,23:This is hard(−:
```

Problem 3.9.6

Consider matrices G and H, both of size 3 × 3

```
G = [1 2 3; 4 5 6; 7 8 9]
H = [11 12 13; 14 15 16; 17 18 19]
```

Replace column 1 of G with row 3 of H using shorthand notation (see Section 3.6).

Problem 3.9.7

Consider matrix I, defined as

```
I = [1:10;11:20;21:30]
```

Empty the last 5 columns of I and call the new matrix J. Empty the first 2 rows of J and call the new matrix K.

Problem 3.9.8

Create a 1 × 4 matrix called L and a 4 × 1 matrix called M. Then concatenate L and M to create one matrix called N of size 1 × 8 and another matrix called O of size 8 × 1.

Problem 3.9.9

Define 2 matrices, Jack and Jill, as follows.

```
Jack = [1:3:35]
Jill = [2:3:36]
```

Create a new matrix, Mary, by replacing every other cell in Jack with the values in the corresponding positions of Jill.

Problem 3.9.10

Define a matrix Up as follows.

```
start_value = 1
step = 2
last_value = 80
Up = [start_value:step:last_value]
```

Define a new value Down that is the mirror image of Up. Check the output carefully and make whatever change is needed to ensure exact mirroring of Up and Down.

4. Calculations

This chapter covers the following topics:

The commands that are introduced and the sections in which they are premiered are as follows:

+	(4.1)
—	(4.1)
*	(4.1)
/	(4.1)
^	(4.1)
abs	(4.2)
exp	(4.2)
log	(4.2)
rem	(4.2)
sqrt	(4.2)
corrcoef	(4.4)
sum	(4.4)
mean	(4.4)
median	(4.4)
polyfit	(4.4)
std	(4.4)
var	(4.4)
NaN	(4.5)
nanmax	(4.5)
nanmean	(4.5)
nanmedian	(4.5)
nanmin	(4.5)
annstd	(4.5)
nansum	(4.5)
nanvar	(4.5)

`.*`	(4.6)
`./`	(4.6)
`.^`	(4.6)
`ceil`	(4.8)
`fix`	(4.8)
`floor`	(4.8)
`max`	(4.8)
`min`	(4.8)
`round`	(4.8)
`sort`	(4.8)
`sortrows`	(4.8)
`rand`	(4.9)
`randn`	(4.9)
`randperm`	(4.9)
`calendar`	(4.10)
`magic`	(4.10)

4.1   Adding, Subtracting, Multiplying, Dividing Values, and Raising Values to a Power

In the last chapter we considered how matrices can be created and accessed with MATLAB. In this chapter we consider how calculations can be performed.

Addition, subtraction, multiplication, and division work in the way you might expect:

Code 4.1.1:

```
a = 1;
b = 2;
c = a + b      % addition
d = 1;
e = c - d      % subtraction
f = 4;
g = f * 3;     % multiplication (note the use of the
                 asterisk, *)
h = f/g        % division
```

Output 4.1.1:

```
c =
     3
e =
     2
h =
     0.333
```

Raising a value to a power is achieved with the caret character (^):

Code 4.1.2:

```
i = 2;
j = 3;
k = i^j   % i raised to the j power
```

Output 4.1.2

```
k =
     8
```

Finding the nth root of a value is also achieved by raising the value to a power. This is possible because the nth root of a value equals the value raised to the $1/n$ power. Thus, the square root of a value is equal to that value raised to the 1/2 power, the cube root of a value is equal to the value raised to the 1/3 power, and so on.

Code 4.1.3:

```
m = 64;
n = 1/2;
p = m^n
```

Output 4.1.3:

```
p = 8
```

It is possible to raise a value to a power expressed in decimal format. Moreover, the power need not be a rational number (a number equal to the ratio of two integers).

Code 4.1.4:

```
pp = 2^.2415
```

Output 4.1.4:

```
pp =
     1.182
```

4.2   Using Built-in Functions to Compute the Square Root, Remainder, Absolute Value, Base of the Natural Logarithms Raised to a Power, and the Logarithm

MATLAB provides a built-in function for taking the square root.

Code 4.2.1:

```
q = sqrt(m)
```

Output 4.2.1:

```
q = 8
```

`rem` returns the remainder after division. This function is valuable for determining whether a value is odd or even. If a value is odd, the remainder after division by 2 is one. However, if a value is even, the remainder after division by 2 is zero. Here we determine what remains after we divide a variable called `subject_number` by 2. In this case, because `subject_number` happens to be 7, the value of the remainder is 1.

Code 4.2.2:

```
subject_number = 7;
remainder = rem(subject_number,2)
```

Output 4.2.2:

```
remainder =
     1
```

As you can imagine, determining whether a subject number is odd or even can be very useful in assigning subjects to conditions in a behavioral science experiment.

`abs` gives the absolute value of a number. Taking the absolute value of a number (also known as *rectifying* the number) makes the value positive if it is negative.

Code 4.2.3:

```
abs(−1)
```

Output 4.2.3:

```
ans =
     1
```

`exp` is used to raise the base of the natural logarithms to a desired power. The base of the natural logarithms is a special value in mathematics, often denoted e. Here e is raised to the 2 power.

Code 4.2.4:

```
k = exp(2)
```

Output 4.2.4:

```
k =
    7.3891
```

As a technical aside, it is useful to ask, what exactly is e? e equals the limit of $(1+1/n)^n$ as n approaches infinity. The value $e^x = exp(x)$ is important because its derivative equals itself. The derivative of a dependent variable with respect to some independent variable equals the amount by which the dependent variable changes as a result of an infinitesimal change in the independent variable. Thus, the derivative of position with respect to time is the amount by which position changes with an infinitesimal change of time. The fact that the derivative of e^x is e^x makes e a convenient quantity for modeling change. It happens that e can be approximated numerically and so can be calculated with a digital computer to a level of precision that is usually adequate for typical behavioral science needs.

Code 4.2.5:

```
exp(1)
```

Output 4.2.5:

```
ans =
    2.7183
```

Although e is the traditional symbol for the base of the natural logarithms, it is not a reserved term in MATLAB.

Code 4.2.6:

```
e = 12
```

Output 4.2.6:

```
e =
    12.000
```

The inverse of `exp` is `log`. Having earlier set `k` to `exp` (2), we can ask what value e is raised to in order to get `k`. The `log` function serves this purpose.

Code 4.2.7:

```
log(k)
```

Output 4.2.7:

```
ans =
      2
```

Later in this chapter we look at the use of `exp` and `log` in connection with matrices that have more than one row or column.

When you give a command like `log(k)`, MATLAB assumes that the base of the logarithm is e. As an aside, when you read technical material and come across a term like ln x, the term ln usually means the "natural logarithm," or logarithm of x to the base e. ln is not a reserved term in MATLAB, however.

Two other bases are permitted when the `log` function is called, namely, 2 and 10.

Code 4.2.8:

```
log2(30)
```

Output 4.2.8:

```
ans =
      4.9069
```

Code 4.2.9:

```
log10(30)
```

Output 4.2.9:

```
ans =           .
      1.4771
```

The use of a base other than e or 2 or 10 is futile if you generalize the syntax of the foregoing examples. Here is an example with the error feedback that follows.

Code 4.2.10:

```
log5(30)
```

Output 4.2.10:

```
> log5(30)
??? Undefined function or variable 'log5'.
```

Nonetheless, other bases can be obtained using the formula

$$\log_b(x) = \log_a(x) / \log_a(b).$$

Thus, log5(30) = log(30) / log(5).

Another important quantity in mathematics, traditionally known as i, is the square root of -1.

Code 4.2.11:

```
sqrt(-1)
```

Output 4.2.11:

```
ans =
      0 + 1.0000i
```

i is an "imaginary" number because the only way to obtain a negative product such as -1 is to multiply a positive number by a negative number $(-1 = 1 \times -1)$, so taking the square root of a negative product like -1 cannot be the same thing as taking the square root of a positive value. Yet i has a geometric interpretation, so even though it is an imaginary number, it is not a non-sensical number: The geometric mean of two variables, a and b, is the square root of their product. Consequently, it is meaningful to consider the geometric mean of 1 and -1. The geometric mean of 1 and -1 is the square root of -1, or i.

Code 4.2.12:

```
imaginary = sqrt(1*-1)
```

Output 4.2.12:

```
imaginary =
      0 + 1.0000i
```

When an imaginary number is scaled by a real number, the product is known as a complex number.

Code 4.2.13:

```
complex = 2*imaginary
```

Output 4.2.13:

```
complex =
      0 + 2.0000i
```

Complex numbers are widely used in engineering research. An advantage of complex numbers is that they let you express the location of a point in a plane with a single complex number. For example, the single complex number $1 + 2i$ defines the location of a point in a plane whose x and y coordinates are 1 and 2, respectively. Knowing this, it is possible to perform algebraic manipulations using complex numbers. For example, you can easily add and subtract complex numbers.

Unless you set *i* to some other value, MATLAB sets *i* to `sqrt(−1)`. You can set *i* to some other value if you wish, but if you do, you must set it back to `sqrt(−1)` if you want to use it for calculations involving complex numbers.

4.3   Ordering Calculations

When you program calculations in MATLAB, you often program more than one calculation per line of code. It is important to be clear about the order of operations. The following example shows that different outputs involving the same values and operations depend on how the calculations are ordered.

Code 4.3.1:

```
r = 2;
s = 3;
t = 4;
u = 5;
v = 6;

w(1) = r * s — t ^ u/v;
w(2) = r * s — (t ^ u)/v;
w(3) = r * (s — t ^ u)/v;
w(4) = r * (s — t) ^ u/v;
w(5) = (r * s) — t ^ u/v;
w(6) = (r * s — t) ^ u/v;
w(7) = (r * s — t) ^ (u/v);
w(8) = ((r * s — t) ^ u)/v;
w(9) = r * (s — t ^ u/v);
w' % list w(1) through w(9) in column form
```

Output 4.3.1:

```
ans =
  −164.6667
  −164.6667
  −340.3333
    −0.3333
  −164.6667
     5.3333
     1.7818
     5.3333
  −335.3333
```

As seen above, the outcomes differ depending on whether parentheses are used and how the parentheses are positioned. MATLAB, like other computer programming languages, has a default ordering of calculations. The ordering is exponentiation first, multiplication and division second, and addition and subtraction third. Even knowing this rule, however, it is a good idea to include parentheses because you can get incorrect results when many calculations are performed in one line. Parentheses can be embedded within other parentheses, as seen in the definition of w(8), given previously. Experienced programmers often type the opening and closing parentheses before typing in any values between them. This helps avoid "parenthesis orphans" which have an opening parenthesis without a closing parenthesis or vice versa. Parenthesis orphans yield error messages, as seen in Output 4.3.2.

Code 4.3.2:

```
w(9) = r * (s — t ^ u/v;
```

Output 4.3.2:

```
??? w(9) = r * (s — t ^ u/v;

Error: Incomplete or malformed expression or statement.
```

4.4   Performing Statistical Calculations to Obtain the Sum, Mean, Standard Deviation, Variance, Correlation, and Least-Squares Fit

MATLAB provides several functions for statistics. These deserve special attention because of the importance of statistics in behavioral science.

Here is a short program that illustrates some of MATLAB's built-in functions relevant to statistics. The program computes the sum, mean, median, standard deviation, and variance of the matrix r, consisting of the numbers 1 through 99.

Code 4.4.1:

```
r = [1:99];
sum_ r = sum(r)
mean_ r = mean(r)
median_ r = median(r)
standard_deviation_ r = std(r)
variance_ r = var(r)
```

Output 4.4.1:

```
sum_ r =
        4950
mean_ r =
        50
median_ r =
        50
standard_deviation_ r =
        28.7228
variance_ r =
        825
```

When you apply the same functions to a multi-row matrix, MATLAB computes the values on a column-by-column basis.

Code 4.4.2:

```
r = [1:4; 11:14];
sum_vector = sum(r)
mean_vector = mean(r)
median_vector = median(r)
standard_deviation_vector = std(r)
variance_vector = var(r)
```

Output 4.4.2:

```
sum_vector =
         12        14        16        18
mean_vector =
          6         7         8         9
median_vector =
          6         7         8         9
standard_deviation_vector =
       7.0711    7.0711    7.0711    7.0711
variance_vector =
         50        50        50        50
```

Another important statistic in behavioral science is the Pearson product-moment correlation coefficient. MATLAB computes this value with `corrcoef`. For technical reasons, `corrcoef` returns a 2 × 2 matrix. (To learn about those technical reasons, you can type `help corrcoef` into the MATLAB command line). You normally need only the top right or bottom left value of this 2 × 2 matrix.

To see how a Pearson product-moment correlation coefficient can be obtained with MATLAB, consider the code below, which specifies two vectors, s and t, that have a perfect negative correlation of −1. Thus, for each increment in s there is a corresponding decrease in t. The lengths of s and t must be the same for the correlation to be computed. In the example, the top right value of `correlation_matrix` is assigned to r. The bottom left value could just as well have been used.

Code 4.4.3:

```
clear r % because it was used in the last example
s = [1:20];
t = [50:−1:31];
correlation_matrix = corrcoef(s,t)
r = correlation_matrix(1,2)
```

Output 4.4.3:

```
correlation_matrix =
      1  −1
     −1   1
r =
     −1
```

Another MATLAB function lets you find the best-fitting line for a scatterplot of data. This function is called `polyfit` and is described in Section 9.9, where `polyfit` is illustrated in connection with plotting data.

4.5   Performing Statistical Calculations With Missing Data

Behavioral science experiments sometimes end up with missing data. MATLAB provides a special value, NaN, and a set of functions, `nanmean`, `nanstd`, `nanvar`, `nansum`, `nanmin`, and `nanmax`, that make missing values less of a nuisance than they might be otherwise.

The value NaN, as its name suggests, is not a number. it is not a literal character, nor is it a string of literal characters (see Chapter 8). Instead, it is a special value in a class by itself, "neither fish nor fowl." Any element of a matrix assigned the value NaN is an element not to be included in summary statistics of ordinary data.

The following program illustrates how NaN can be assigned to the elements of a matrix and how statistics can then be obtained from the matrix in a way that leaves out the NaN values.

Code 4.5.1:

```
% NaN_Calculations_01
% August 7, 2006

clc
clear all

% Review of special numbers other than NaN, pi, and i.
% Reminder that the default value of i can be overwritten
% but can then be restored by clearing i
The_Special_Number_Pi = pi
The_Special_Number_Sqrt_Minus_1 = i
i = 10;
i _Redefined = i
Not_Really_The_Special_Number_Sqrt_Minus_1 = i
clear i
After_Clearing_The_Special_Number_Sqrt_Minus_1 = i
```

```
% Blank_Slate filled with NaN at first, but then gets
% some data and is finally assigned to Slate_With_Data
Blank_Slate(1:4,1:4) = NaN
Blank_Slate(1,2:4) = [7 8 9];
Blank_Slate(2,1:3) = [6 7 8];
Blank_Slate(3,3:4) = [10 11];
Blank_Slate(4,1) = [12];
Slate_With_Data = Blank_Slate

% Statistics
Column_Means = nanmean(Slate_With_Data)
Column_Standard_Deviations = nanstd(Slate_With_Data)

commandwindow
```

Output 4.5.1:

```
The_Special_Number_Pi =
    3.1416

The_Special_Number_Sqrt_Minus_1 =
    0 + 1.0000i

i_Redefined =
    10

Not_Really_The_Special_Number_Sqrt_Minus_1 =
    10

After_Clearing_The_Special_Number_Sqrt_Minus_1 =
    0 + 1.0000i

Blank_Slate =
    NaN NaN NaN NaN
    NaN NaN NaN NaN
    NaN NaN NaN NaN
    NaN NaN NaN NaN

Slate_With_Data =
    NaN 7   8   9
    6   7   8   NaN
    NaN NaN 10  11
    12  NaN NaN NaN

Column_Means =
    9.0000  7.0000  8.6667  10.0000
```

```
Column_Standard_Deviations =
        4.2426   0 1.1547      1.4142
```

4.6   Calculating With Matrices

Earlier in this chapter, you learned about addition, subtraction, multiplication, division, and exponentiation for single values. Recall that a single value can be viewed as a matrix of size [1 1]. MATLAB also lets you carry out calculations with larger matrices.

Code 4.6.1:

```
u = [1:6]
v = u + 20
```

Output 4.6.1:

```
u =
     1    2    3    4    5    6
v =
    21   22   23   24   25   26
```

A number can also be subtracted from a matrix.

Code 4.6.2:

```
w = v − 20
```

Output 4.6.2:

```
w =
     1    2    3    4    5    6
```

A matrix can be multiplied by a number.

Code 4.6.3:

```
x = w * 2
```

Output 4.6.3:

```
x =
     2    4    6    8   10   12
```

A matrix can be divided by a number.

Code 4.6.4:

```
y = x / 2
```

Output 4.6.4:

```
y =
     1    2    3    4    5    6
```

A number can be added to each element of a multi-row matrix.

Code 4.6.5:

```
Z1 = [1:6;7:12]
Z2 = Z1 + 2
```

Output 4.6.5:

```
Z1 =
     1    2    3    4    5    6
     7    8    9   10   11   12
Z2 =
     3    4    5    6    7    8
     9   10   11   12   13   14
```

When two matrices are added, the elements in the same positions are summed.

Code 4.6.6:

```
Z3 = Z1 + Z2
```

Output 4.6.6:

```
Z3 =
     4    6    8   10   12   14
    16   18   20   22   24   26
```

The same holds for subtraction.

Code 4.6.7:

```
Z4 = Z1 - 2
Z5 = Z1 - Z2
```

Output 4.6.7:

```
Z4 =
       -1    0    1    2    3    4
        5    6    7    8    9   10

Z5 =
       -2   -2   -2   -2   -2   -2
       -2   -2   -2   -2   -2   -2
```

The .* operator multiplies matrices element by element, allowing you to take the products of the values in corresponding row and column positions.

Code 4.6.8:

```
aa = [1:4;5:8]
bb = [4:-1:1;8:-1:5]
cc = aa .* bb
```

Output 4.6.8:

```
aa =
        1    2    3    4
        5    6    7    8

bb =
        4    3    2    1
        8    7    6    5

cc =
        4    6    6    4
       40   42   42   40
```

Likewise, the ./ operator performs element-by-element division.

Code 4.6.9:

```
dd = aa ./ bb
```

Output 4.6.9:

```
dd =
       0.2500   0.6667   1.5000   4.0000
       0.6250   0.8571   1.1667   1.6000
```

Similarly, the .^ operator raises each element of a matrix to an exponent:

Code 4.6.10:

```
dd = aa .^ .25
```

Output 4.6.10:

```
dd =
        1.0000    1.1892    1.3161   11.4142
        1.4953    1.5651    1.6266    1.6818
```

4.7   Using Matrix Algebra

MATLAB lets you perform calculations with pairs of matrices using *, ^, and / without putting a dot before each symbol. When you perform such calculations, you enter the world of matrix algebra, a world unfamiliar to many behavioral scientists. Because it is not feasible for a book like this to cover matrix algebra, I have elected to omit a review of what can be done with "dotless" *, ^, and /. This is ironic in view of the fact that the word MATLAB actually is shorthand for "matrix laboratory." If you are familiar with matrix algebra and have grasped the material given above, you should have little trouble learning the many ways that MATLAB can be used to perform the full range of calculations in matrix algebra. Use MATLAB help to delve into this topic. You can begin by typing help *.

4.8   Obtaining the Max, Min, Sort, Round, Floor, and Ceiling

It is easy to find the largest value of a matrix.

Code 4.8.1:

```
array = [−1:.5:1];
max(array)
```

Output 4.8.1:

```
ans =
     1
```

For a multi-row matrix like dd, max gives the maximum of each column.

Code 4.8.2:

```
max(dd)
```

Output 4.8.2:

```
ans =
     1.4953     1.5651     1.6266     1.6818
```

Not surprisingly, it is also easy to find the smallest value of a matrix.

Code 4.8.3:

```
min(array)
```

Output 4.8.3:

```
ans =
     -1
```

For a multi-row matrix like dd, min gives the minimum of each column.

Code 4.8.4:

```
min(dd)
```

Output 4.8.4:

```
ans =
     1.0000   1.1892   1.3161   1.4142
```

You can also sort values in ascending order by using the sort function.

Code 4.8.5:

```
r = [3 2 1]
sorted_r = sort(r)
```

Output 4.8.5:

```
r =
     3    2    1

sorted_ r =
     1    2    3
```

For a matrix with more than one column, you can sort several columns with a single command. Here a matrix is sorted based on two sets of random numbers. Random number generators are premiered more fully in section 4.8.

Code 4.8.6:

```
rr = [rand(10,1) randperm(10)']
srr1 = sort(rr)
```

Output 4.8.6:

```
rr =
        0.1870     3.0000
        0.9913     2.0000
        0.7120     8.0000
        0.8714    10.0000
        0.4796     9.0000
        0.4960     4.0000
        0.2875     7.0000
        0.0609     5.0000
        0.2625     6.0000
        0.1863     1.0000

srr1 =
        0.0609     1.0000
        0.1863     2.0000
        0.1870     3.0000
        0.2625     4.0000
        0.2875     5.0000
        0.4796     6.0000
        0.4960     7.0000
        0.7120     8.0000
        0.8714     9.0000
        0.9913    10.0000
```

You can sort by one column at a time. Here column 1 is sorted in ascending order, yielding srr2, and then column 2 is sorted in ascending order, yielding srr3.

Code 4.8.7:

```
srr2 = sortrows(rr,1)
srr3 = sortrows(rr,2)
```

Output 4.8.7:

```
srr2 =
        0.0609     5.0000
        0.1863     1.0000
        0.1870     3.0000
        0.2625     6.0000
        0.2875     7.0000
        0.4796     9.0000
        0.4960     4.0000
        0.7120     8.0000
        0.8714    10.0000
        0.9913     2.0000

srr3 =
        0.1863     1.0000
        0.9913     2.0000
        0.1870     3.0000
        0.4960     4.0000
        0.0609     5.0000
        0.2625     6.0000
        0.2875     7.0000
        0.7120     8.0000
        0.4796     9.0000
        0.8714    10.0000
```

To obtain a list of indices of sorted values in addition to the sorted values themselves, you can use code like the following. The values in the output matrix, Y, are the values in the two columns of rr sorted from smallest to largest, just as when you simply use the command $sort(rr)$. The other output values, ranked rr, are the indices of the items within their respective columns. (Note that this is the first time you have seen a function yielding an output with more than one value. In Chapter 8, more is said about multiple outputs from functions.)

Code 4.8.8:

```
[Y, ranked_rr] = sort(rr)
```

Output 4.8.8:

```
Y =
        0.0609      1.0000
        0.1863      2.0000
        0.1870      3.0000
        0.2625      4.0000
        0.2875      5.0000
        0.4796      6.0000
        0.4960      7.0000
        0.7120      8.0000
        0.8714      9.0000
        0.9913     10.0000

ranked_rr =
        8          10
       10           2
        1           1
        9           6
        7           8
        5           9
        6           7
        3           3
        4           5
        2           4
```

MATLAB lets you round down to the nearest integer if the value to the right of the decimal point is less than or equal to .5, and it lets you round up to the nearest integer if the value to the right of the decimal point is greater than .5.

Code 4.8.9:

```
round(dd)
```

Output 4.8.9:

```
ans =
     1    1    1    1
     1    2    2    2
```

MATLAB also lets you truncate to the next lowest integer regardless of the value to the right of the decimal point using the floor function.

Code 4.8.10:

```
floor(dd)
```

Output 4.8.10:

```
ans =
     1   1   1   1
     1   1   1   1
```

You can raise values to the next highest integer regardless of what number appears to the right of the decimal point by using the `ceil` function.

Code 4.8.11:

```
ceil(dd)
```

Output 4.8.11:

```
ans =
     2   2   2   2
     2   2   2   2
```

You can bring values to the next closest integer toward zero regardless of what number appears to the right of the decimal point by using the `fix` function. Here `fix` is applied both to dd and −dd. Meanwhile, `floor` is applied to −dd to show how the output differs when `floor` or `fix` is applied to negative values.

Code 4.8.12:

```
fix_dd = fix(dd)
fix_minus_dd = fix(−dd)
floor_minus_dd = floor(−dd)
```

Output 4.8.11:

```
fix_dd =
      1    1    1    1
      1    1    1    1

fix_minus_dd =
     −1   −1   −1   −1
     −1   −1   −1   −1

floor_minus_dd =
     −1   −2   −2   −2
     −2   −2   −2   −2
```

4.9   Generating Random Numbers

In doing simulations and conducting experiments in which you want events to be unpredict-able, it is useful to generate random numbers. MATLAB provides several random number generators.

The `rand` function generates uniformly distributed random numbers within the range 0 to 1. Random numbers that are uniformly distributed in some range such as 0 to 1 are equally likely to appear anywhere within the range. Here we assign uniformly distributed random numbers to the cells of a 2 × 5 matrix (one such number to a cell). The instruction that achieves the assignment is the second line of Code 4.8.1. The first line of Code 4.8.1 initializes `rand` to an arbitrary state.

Code 4.9.1:

```
rand('state',sum(100*clock));
rand(2,5)
```

Output 4.9.1:

```
ans =
      0.9501    0.6068    0.8913    0.4565    0.8214
      0.2311    0.4860    0.7621    0.0185    0.4447
```

The `randn` function, in contrast to the `rand` function, generates normally distributed ran-dom numbers. Normally distributed numbers are described by a bell shape with approxi-mately 68% of its values within ±1 standard deviation of the mean. By default, `randn` uses a mean of 0 and a standard deviation of 1. Consequently, the generated numbers tend to be close to the mean of 0. The code that follows shows how to assign normally distributed ran-dom numbers to cells in a 2 × 5 matrix. As before, the first line initializes the randomization to an arbitrary state.

Code 4.9.2:

```
randn('state',sum(100*clock));
randn(2,5)
```

Output 4.9.2:

```
ans =
     -0.4326    0.1253   -1.1465    1.1892    0.3273
     -1.6656    0.2877    1.1909   -0.0376    0.1746
```

You can generate another matrix of normally distributed numbers with a mean, `mu`, of 10 and a standard deviation, `stdev`, of 15.

Code 4.9.3:

```
randn('state',sum(100*clock));
mu = 10;
stdev = 15;
new_distribution = mu + (randn(2,5)*stdev)
```

Output 4.9.3:

```
new_distribution =
   -14.0613    -5.8471    -2.0764    13.2898   -22.5601
    13.8596    31.2271    17.9311    -3.8285     9.1122
```

The `randperm` function lets you generate a random permutation of a specified number of items. This can be extremely useful in experimental designs where, for example, you want to assign treatments to participants on a random basis. Thus, if a participant in an experiment is to receive 8 different treatments, the assignment of treatments to that participant can be generated as follows.

Code 4.9.4:

```
r = randperm(8)
```

Output 4.9.4:

```
r =
     5    6    1    4    2    8    3    7
```

4.10 Generating Magic Squares and Calendars

Many tutorials about MATLAB feature the "magic square"—a matrix of size n × n such that all the elements in each row and column sum to the same value. MATLAB provides a function called `magic` for generating such matrices.

Code 4.10.1:

```
n = 4;
magic(n)
```

Output 4.10.1:

```
ans =
    16     2     3    13
     5    11    10     8
     9     7     6    12
     4    14    15     1
```

Another built-in function that may be more useful is `calendar`. The `calendar` command by itself gives the calendar for the present month. To get the calendar for a specific year and month, say July 1776, the syntax is as follows:

Code 4.10.2:

```
calendar(1776,7)
```

Output 4.10.2:

```
Jul 1776
        S    M   Tu    W   Th    F    S
        0    1    2    3    4    5    6
        7    8    9   10   11   12   13
       14   15   16   17   18   19   20
       21   22   23   24   25   26   27
       28   29   30   31    0    0    0
        0    0    0    0    0    0    0
```

Through this procedure, we learn that the American Declaration of Independence was signed on a Thursday.

4.11   Practicing Calculations

Try your hand at the following exercises, using only the methods introduced so far in this book or information given in the problems themselves.

Problem 4.11.1

You have done a study on the effects of five different treatments on the performance of two groups of participants. One group had earlier exposure to the task, causing their mean score to be 15 points higher than was the case for the first-time group. The data for the two groups are as follows:

```
First_Time_Group = [71 78 80 86  91]
Second_Time_Group = [86 91 97 97 110]
```

What single line of code will remove the 15 point advantage for the Second_Time_Group?

Problem 4.11.2

Continuing with the study of the two groups and using the original values of First_Time_Group and the transformed value of Second_Time_Group, compute the mean and standard deviation of First_Time_Group, the mean and standard deviation of Second_Time_Group, and the mean and standard deviation of the paired differences between First_Time_Group and Second_Time_Group. Use variable names that make it easy to understand the output.

Problem 4.11.3

Assign random permutations of 8 treatments, numbered 1 to 8, to each of 4 participants.

Problem 4.11.4

Amy participated in a gymnastics competition. She received the following scores in each of 4 events.

    Vault: 8.9, 8.7, 8.2, 9.1, 9.0
    Uneven_bar: 9.5, 9.3, 9.3, 9.25, 8.9
    Balance_beam: 8.9, 8.9, 8.7, 8.6, 8.5
    Floor: 8.9, 8.8, 8.8, 8.7, 8.9

Amy's final score for any given event needs to be the mean score after removing the lowest and highest score for that event. Write a program that computes Amy's final score in each apparatus and then the total of all her final scores.

Problem 4.11.5

You are preparing stimuli for an experiment and discover a mistake in the final column of values on which the stimuli will be based. Each value in the final column needs to be squared. Write a program to correct the error. Don't just square each mistaken value by hand. The data that need to be corrected are as follows:

```
Data_Needing_Correction = [23 24 5; 34 35 6; 46 47 7]
```

5. Contingencies

This chapter covers the following topics:

The commands that are introduced and the sections in which they are premiered are as follows:

`==`	(5.1)
`>`	(5.1)
`>=`	(5.1)
`|`	(5.1)
`<`	(5.1)
`<=`	(5.1)
`~=`	(5.1)
`Ctrl-]`	(5.1)
`Ctrl-`	(5.1)
`else`	(5.1)
`elseif`	(5.1)
`end`	(5.1)
`if`	(5.1)
`case`	(5.2)
`otherwise`	(5.2)
`switch`	(5.2)
`for`	(5.3)
`break`	(5.4)
`Ctrl-C`	(5.4)
`while`	(5.4)
`tic`	(5.5)
`toc`	(5.5)
`find`	(5.7)

5.1   **Using the** `if … else … end` **Construct**

Computer programs handle contingencies. That is, they allow for different actions depending on different conditions. This single fact about computers could be considered their defining feature. Their great speed, in contrast, could be considered one of their characteristic features. As one author once said, the quality that distinguishes a computer from an adding machine is that the computer can do "ifs."

Here is an example using `if … else … end`. The program dictates that if a equals 1 (one condition), b should be multiplied by 2 (an action), but if a does not equal 1 (another condition), b should be multiplied by –2 (another action).

Code 5.1.1:

```
b = 2;
a = 1;
if a == 1
     b = 2 * b;
else
     b = −2 * b;
end
b
```

Output 5.1.1:

```
b =
     4
```

Notice that a double equal sign was needed in `a == 1`. A single equal sign in `if` statements yields an error message. The reason is that in MATLAB a double equal sign denotes comparison, whereas a single equal sign denotes assignment.

The program also required an `else` statement to tell MATLAB what to do if a did not equal 1. The program concluded with `end`, which is mandatory after an `if` statement, regardless of whether there is an `else` as well.

Suppose you don't want to do anything if a does not equal 1. In that case, you can omit the `else` command as well as the command after it. Thus, `else` is optional.

Code 5.1.2:

```
b = 2;
a = −1;
if a == 1
     b = 2 * b;
end
b
```

Output 5.1.2:

```
b =
     2
```

In the next example, b gets different values if a is negative, if a equals 0, or if a equals 1. The elseif command is useful in this context.

Code 5.1.3:

```
b = 2;
a = 1;
if a < 0
     b = -1;
elseif a == 0
     b = 0;
elseif a == 1
     b = 1;
end
b
```

Output 5.1.3:

```
b =
1
```

Next, we check whether a is greater than or equal to 1 and less than or equal to 3. We must list each of these criteria separately, in contrast to the way we describe the criteria in everyday English, as in the opening sentence of the previous sentence. We use >= to specify greater than or equal, & to specify and, and <= to specify less than or equal to. The parentheses in the if statement help clarify the intended parsing.

Code 5.1.4:

```
b = 2;
a = 2.7;
if (a >= 1) & (a <= 3)
     b = 2 * b
end
```

Output 5.1.4:

```
b =
4
```

In the next example we check whether a is less than or equal to 1 or greater than or equal to 3. We use the | symbol to specify or. The value of b is unchanged if neither condition is met.

Code 5.1.5:

```
b = 2;
a = 3.7;
if (a <= 1) | (a >= 3)
    b = -b;
end
b
```

Output 5.1.5:

```
b =
-2
```

It is worth mentioning that the | symbol specifies just one kind of disjunction, namely, "logical or." When | is used in the above example, the condition is satisfied if *either* a <= 1 or a >= 3. For information about other versions of or supported by MATLAB, type help or in the MATLAB command line.

In the next example we check whether a is not equal to 10. We use the ~= symbol for this purpose.

Code 5.1.6:

```
b = -2;
a = 3.7;
if a ~= 10
    b = -b;
end
b
```

Output 5.1.6:

```
b =
2
```

Nesting of if statements allows for more complex contingencies.

Code 5.1.7:

```
A = -2.3
a = 10
if A <= 0
     if a <= -5
          b = 1;   %if A is <=0 and if a <=-5, b gets 1
     else
          b = 2;   %if A is <=0 and if a is not <=-5,
                   % b gets 2
     end
else
     if a <= 5
          b = 3;   %if A is not <=0 and if a <=5, b gets 3
     else
          b = 4;   %if A is not <=0 and if a is not <=5,
                   % b gets 4
     end
end
b
```

Output 5.1.7:

```
A =
     -2.3000
a =
     10
b =
     2
```

Notice that the foregoing program used indentation to accentuate the nesting. Indentation occurs automatically if you turn on Smart indent through the MATLAB command window. The way to do this is to follow the path File → Editor/Debugging. Other options exist for configuring code (see Chapter 2).

You can also select a block of text and indent it using Ctrl–]. This keypress combination moves a selected block of text to the right to a previously defined tab position. Alternatively, you can outdent a select block of text with Ctrl–[. This keypress combination moves the selected text to the *left*, to a previously defined tab position.

5.2   **Using the** `switch … case … end` **Construct**

There is an alternative to `if … else … end`, namely `switch … case … end`. Using `switch … case … end` is a convenient way to compare a single variable against a number of possible values. Here is an example in which different actions are taken depending on the value of x. In case x equals 1, y is set to -1; in case x equals 2, y is set to $-2*x$; and so on.

Code 5.2.1:

```
x = 1;
switch x
    case 1
        y = -1;
    case 2
        y = -2*x;
    case 3
        y = -3*x;
    otherwise
        y = 0;
end
```

Output 5.2.1:

```
y =
    -1
```

Here is another example of the `switch … case … end` construct. This program indicates the number of days in any given month and was kindly provided by Hank Heijink.

Code 5.2.2:

```
% Days_In_A_Month
month = 4;    % April, but choose any month
year = 2006; % 2006, but choose any year
switch month
    case {4, 6, 9, 11}
        no_of_days = 30;
    case 2
        if rem(year, 4) == 0 & …
            (rem(year, 100) ~= 0 | rem(year, 400) == 0)
            % it is a leap year
            no_of_days = 29;
        else
        no_of_days = 28;
        end
    otherwise
        no_of_days = 31;
end
[year month no_of_days]  % display result in matrix form
```

Output 5.2.2:

```
ans =
2006      4          30
```

5.3   Using the `for … end` Construct

The `for` loop lets you perform operations over and over, for as many times as you specify.

In this example, 2 is multiplied by the variable `i`, which takes on the values of 1, 2, 3, 4, 5, or 6. The `for` loop concludes with an `end` statement.

Code 5.3.1:

```
for i = 1:6
    a = 2 * i
end
```

Output 5.3.1:

```
a =
      2
a =
      4
a =
      6
a =
      8
a =
     10
a =
     12
```

In the next example, we add a semicolon to the second line to suppress immediate output. In addition and more crucially, `i` also serves as the index for `a`. Thus, column 1 of `a` gets the product of 2×1, column 2 of `a` gets the product of 2×2, and so on.

Code 5.3.2:

```
for i = 1:6
    a(i) = 2 * i;
end
a
```

Output 5.3.2:

```
a =
2     4    6    8    10   12
```

It is also easy to use a for loop to create a more complex matrix. In this example we set the element in the `i`-th row and `j`-th column of matrix `a` to `i + j`.

Code 5.3.3:

```
for i = 1:6
    for j = 1:3
        a(i,j) = i + j;
    end
end
a
```

Output 5.3.3:

```
a =
     2    3    4    8   10   12
     3    4    5    0    0    0
     4    5    6    0    0    0
     5    6    7    0    0    0
     6    7    8    0    0    0
     7    8    9    0    0    0
```

Something odd happened in Output 5.3.3. We expected a matrix with 6 rows and 3 columns but ended up with a matrix of size 6 × 6. What happened?

The answer is that a was not cleared from before. Its value remained from Output 5.3.2. I include this example as a reminder that MATLAB incorporates new results into a matrix if that matrix is still active. To prevent this from happening (when it is not desired), it is advisable to clear the matrix that will be fully redefined. Here is the same code as in the last example but with a cleared at the beginning.

Code 5.3.4:

```
clear a
for i = 1:6
    for j = 1:3
        a(i,j) = i + j;
    end
end
a
```

Output 5.3.4:

```
a =
     2    3    4
     3    4    5
     4    5    6
     5    6    7
     6    7    8
     7    8    9
```

When you create matrix indices using `for` loops, you must be careful to use positive integers. The following code produces an error.

Code 5.3.5:

```
for i = 0:10
    a(i) = i + 1;
end
```

Output 5.3.5:

```
??? Subscript indices must either be real positive
integers or logicals.
Error in ==> D:\Lab and Teach\PSU Teaching\Programming
Seminar\Programming Seminar .m files\for_bad_index.m
On line 2 ==> a(i) = i+1;
```

The problem is that the first time a value was assigned to the i-th element of a, i equaled 0, but a matrix cannot have a zero-th element. The first element must have an index of 1, the second element must have an index of 2, and so. (The Error message gives the complete directory address and name of this program, which is `for_bad_index.m`.)

Lest you conclude that negative numbers and 0 must be avoided in the context of `for` loops, consider this example, where i takes on values that are negative and, in one pass through the `for` loop, i is equal to 0. These values of i can be used in calculations even though they cannot be used as index values.

Code 5.3.6:

```
x = 10;      '
for i = −3:3
    a = x*i
end
```

Output 5.3.6:

```
a =
      −30
a =
      −20
a =
      −10
a =
        0
a =
       10
a =
       20
a =
       30
```

The following example shows that you can use `for` and `if` together. These elements are combined in the following program, where division of x by i is allowed only if i does not equal zero.

Code 5.3.7:

```
x = 10;
for i = -3:3
      if i ~= 0
            a = x/i
      end
end
```

Output 5.3.7:

```
a =
      -3.3333
a =
      -5
a =
      -10
a =
      10
a =
      5
a =
      3.3333
```

What happens if you do not include the `if` statement in the last example?

Code 5.3.8:

```
x = 10;
for i = -3:3
%      if i ~= 0
            a = x/i
%      end
end
a
```

Output 5.3.8:

```
a =
    -3.3333
a =
    -5
a =
    -10
Warning: Divide by zero.
(Type "warning off MATLAB:divideByZero" to suppress this
warning.)
> In D:\Lab and Teach\PSU Teaching\Programming
Seminar\Programming Seminar .m
files\David_If_For_While_12.m at line 267
a =
    Inf
a =
    10
a =
    5
a =
    3.3333
a =
    3.3333
```

MATLAB forgives you for dividing by zero but some other programming languages don't. Dividing by zero causes programs to come to a grinding halt or, worse, causes computers to crash. Despite MATLAB's forgiveness, it is wise not to divide by zero. Doing so may spoil your outputs (text or graphs) and can give crazy, or at least unexpected, results.

5.4   Using the while … end Construct and Escaping From Runaway Loops

The while … end construct lets you perform operations for as long as a given condition holds. while … end is particularly helpful when it is hard to know how many steps will be needed for a condition to change state. Here is an example. The value of a is updated as long as a remains below 10.

Code 5.4.1:

```
a = 1;
b = .25;
steps = 0;
while a < 10
    a = a + a^b;
    steps = steps + 1;
end
a
steps
```

Output 5.4.1:

```
a =
     10.9475
steps =
     7
```

The `while` loop can be dangerous, however. When using `while`, you can get caught in an endless loop, as in the following program.

Code 5.4.2:

```
a = .75;
need_to_keep_going = 1;
while need_to_keep_going == 1
     a = a^2
     if a > 1
          need_to_keep_going = 0;
     end
end
```

Here we first set `need_to_keep_going` to 1 to create the condition under which the `while` loop was sustained. Then we squared the value of `a`, which was initially set to .75. We believed, innocently but incorrectly, that squaring a value always makes it bigger, so we expected that `a` would grow as it was squared over and over again until it exceeded 1. We indicated that `a` should be squared `while need_to_keep_going == 1`. (Notice that we used a double equal sign in this statement.) We thought that when `a` exceeded 1, `need_to_keep_going` would get 0 and the condition needed to satisfy the `while` loop (`need_to_keep_going == 1`) would no longer be met, in which case the `while` loop would be escaped. The output was not what was expected, however. (Notice that it has been suppressed here.) Rather than seeing a compact list of values that climbed to 1 and then stopped, MATLAB spewed forth a series of values that quickly got so close to zero that all that was visible was `a = 0`, over and over again.

Thankfully, there is a way to terminate runaway programs. As mentioned in Chapter 2, you can hold down the Ctrl and C keys simultaneously on a PC or the flower and C keys simultaneously on a Mac and the program will stop and give an error message.

It is not a good idea to get in the habit of relying on Ctrl-C or flower-C to escape from endless loops (or from long listings of matrices caused by omission of semicolons). It is better to get into the habit of putting a semicolon at the end of every line so outputs are suppressed by default. More importantly it is good to think carefully and plan ahead to avoid runaway programs and other computationally unpleasant events.

One way to prevent endless loops when using `while` is to let the program run through only a set number of steps, as in the following example.

Code 5.4.3:

```
a = .75;
need_to_keep_going = 1;
allowed_steps = 5;
steps = 0;
while (steps < allowed_steps) & (need_to_keep_going == 1)
     a = a^2
     steps = steps + 1;
     if a > 1
          need_to_keep_going = 0;
     end
end
```

Output 5.4.3:

```
a =
     0.5625
a =
     0.3164
a =
     0.1001
a =
     0.0100
a =
     1.0045e—004
```

Another strategy is to use the break command.

Code 5.4.4:

```
a = .75;
 need_to_keep_going = 1;
 step = 0;
 allowed_steps = 1000;
 while need_to_keep_going == 1
     a = a^2;
     if a > 1
          need_to_keep_going = 0;
     end
     step = step + 1;
     if step == allowed_steps
          break
     end
end
a
```

Output 5.4.4:

```
a =
     0
step =
     1000
```

When the `break` command is invoked, the program breaks out of the `while` loop containing it.

5.5 Vectorizing Rather Than Using `for ... end`

Earlier in this chapter you were introduced to `for` loops. These are useful, especially when `if` statements are nested within them (as in Code 5.3.7 and Code 5.3.8), or when other `for` loops are nested within them (as in Code 5.3.3 and Code 5.3.4). However, `for` loops run slowly relative to instructions that can be completed in one fell swoop. The term used in the MATLAB programming community for giving such all-in-one instructions is *vectorizing*. When instructions are vectorized, processing time can be greatly reduced.

You have already been exposed to vectorizing, although the term wasn't introduced before. In chapters 3 and 4 (before the `for` loop was introduced), values were assigned to matrices in single statements. For example, in Code 3.6.2, the values [1:6] were assigned to a matrix M simply by writing M = [1:6]. This is an example of vectorizing. It turns out that it takes less time to assign the values 1 through 6 to the first 6 elements of M by vectorizing than by using a `for` loop and saying, via code, "if the current index is 1, then M(1) gets 1, if the current index is 2, then M(2) gets 2, and so on." For very small matrices the time difference is immaterial, but for larger matrices or for more complex calculations vectorizing can make a noticeable difference.

Here is an example that shows how much more slowly `for` loops can take than vectorizing. The program that achieves the demonstration uses a stopwatch function provided in MATLAB. The stopwatch function is embodied in the `tic ... toc` construct. As its name suggests, `tic` starts a clock (or reads a clock in the computer) and `toc` stops the clock (or reads the computer clock and gives the time difference). The value of the time difference is reported in seconds. The program below yields an output that shows it takes much more time to assign values to a matrix with a `for` loop than it does to assign the same values to a matrix by vectorizing.

Code 5.5.1

```
clear all
n = 50000;
a = 2;

% Multiply using for … end
tic
for i = 1:n
    x(i) = a*i;
end
For_Time = toc

% Multiply using vectorizing
tic
y = a*[1:n];
Vectorize_Time = toc
```

Output 5.5.1

```
For_Time =
      19.3270
Vectorize_Time =
       0
```

According to the output, `For_Time` took 19.327 seconds, whereas `Vectorize_Time` took no time at all. Of course, `Vectorize_Time` was not literally 0 seconds. No computer is that fast! The number was rounded down from the actual (extremely short) time.

The point of this example is not to discourage you from using `for` loops in all cases, because `for` loops can sometimes be easier to understand than vectorizing (especially for people relatively new to MATLAB). Furthermore, in some cases `for` loops are essential (e.g., when `if` loops or other `for` loops are nested within them). Nonetheless, `for` loops should be used judiciously.

5.6   If-ing Instantly

Just as assignments can be achieved without one-at-a-time instructions, comparisons can be achieved in single statements. I call this *if-ing instantly*. I should say immediately that *if-ing* is not an established MATLAB term nor a commonly used computer-programming expression. It is a term I use in my teaching, mainly to spice up the conversation.

Here is a program that contrasts two different methods for making comparisons. The comparisons are used to find values that are larger than the mean of the values in a normally distributed random sample. Comparisons are first made by using a `for` loop with an `if` statement nested within it: For the i-th value of `sample`, if that value is greater than the mean of `sample`, it is added to a matrix called `top_half`. This is the familiar way of making comparisons, reflecting material presented earlier in this chapter.

The second way of making the comparisons is to engage in instant if-ing. This is done here by creating a matrix called `truth_values_of_indices_satisfying_crite-rion`, to which are assigned 1's and 0's. A value of 1 is assigned to the i-th position of this matrix if the i-th value of `sample` exceeds the mean of `sample`. Alternatively, a value of 0 is assigned to the i-th position of the matrix if the i-th value of `sample` does not exceed the mean of `sample`. All the 1's and 0's are assigned on the basis of a single instruction. The actual values that exceed `mean(sample)` are next identified in just one more instruction. A matrix called `new_top_half` is assigned the values of sample whose indices were assigned 1's in the instruction above it. As seen in the output, `new_top_half` and `top_half` are the same.

Code 5.6.1

```
% generate normally distributed random sample
randn('state',sum(100*clock));
sample = randn(1,10);
random_sample = sample' % print out transpose for easy
                        % reading

% identify values greater than the mean using for and if
top_half = [ ];
for i = 1:length(sample)
    if sample(i) > mean(sample)
        top_half = [top_half sample(i)];
    end
end
top_half

% Identify values greater than the mean using instant
% if-ing
truth_values_of_indices_satisfying_criterion = …
[sample > mean(sample)]
new_top_half = …
sample(truth_values_of_indices_satisfying_criterion)
```

Output 5.6.1

```
random_sample =
    -0.0190
     1.1116
     2.6756
    -0.4239
     1.5166
    -0.1902
     0.1163
     1.2005
     0.4585
    -0.5133

top_half =
     1.1116    2.6756    1.5166    1.2005

truth_values_of_indices_satisfying_criterion =
     0   1   1   0   1   0   0   1   0   0

new_top_half =
     1.1116    2.6756    1.5166    1.2005
```

5.7   If-ing Instantly Once Again and Finding Indices of Satisfying Values

Code 5.7.1 provides an example of instant if-ing to illustrate another type of construction. The matrix h is assigned the numbers 1 through 11, which are randomly permuted and added to 10. Then, a new, unnamed, matrix is assigned 1's for elements of h that are equal to 12 or 16. Notice that the == symbol is used for these comparisons and | is used to denote "or."

The third line of Code 5.7.1 introduces a new function, find. This function returns the indices that satisfy the condition given as an argument to the find function. In this case the condition is that elements of h are equal either to 12 or to 16. The find function can be useful for determining which participants satisfied one or more conditions in an experiment. You will have the chance to explore this capability in the exercises to come.

Code 5.7.1

```
h = randperm(11) + 10
(h == 12 | h == 16)
find(h == 12 | h == 16)
```

Output 5.7.1

```
h =
    12   16   15   19   21   11   20   18   14   13   17
ans =
     1    1    0    0    0    0    0    0    0    0    0
ans =
     1    2
```

5.8   Practicing Contingencies

Try your hand at the following exercises, using only the methods introduced so far in this book or in information given in the problems themselves.

Problem 5.8.1

You want to show stimuli to a participant in a psychophysics experiment. The stimuli to be shown should have values drawn from a normal distribution with standard deviation equal to .1 and mean equal to A^B, where A take on the values of 1, 2, 3, and 4, and B takes on values of 1, 2, 3, and 4. Write a program to generate the 16 stimulus values.

Problem 5.8.2

The following matrix contains fictional data from a reaction time experiment. Each row contains the mean reaction time and proportion correct for a different participant. Use a `for` loop and an `if` statement to identify the participants who had mean reaction times greater than 500 ms and proportions correct greater than .65. The output should contain two matrices, called `Identified_Participants` and `OK_Scores`. The values in `Identified_Participants` should be the numbers of the participants fulfilling the criteria. The values in `OK_Scores` should be rows, each with two columns, one column for reaction time and one for proportion correct.

```
RT_and_PC_Data = [
            390             .45
            347             .32
            866             .98
            549             .67
            589             .72
            641             .50
            777             .77
            702             .68
            ];
```

Problem 5.8.3

Use `find` instead of a `for` loop and an `if` statement to solve the last problem. Build on Code 5.6.1.

Problem 5.8.4

Adapt Code 5.6.1 to find out how long it takes your computer to identify values greater than the mean using `for` and `if` statements, and how long it takes your computer to identify values greater than the mean through instant if-ing. The sample should have 10000 values. Suppress output except for the times.

Problem 5.8.5

You are curious to know how many trials it takes a participant to get a certain number of correct responses in a categorization task. You are especially interested to know how the trials to criterion depend on the participant's learning rate. Suppose there are four category names whose corresponding stimuli are each presented an equal number of times. Suppose also that participants are told the correct response after each response. Suppose finally that the probability of a correct response is a logarithmic function of the number of completed trials, according to the equation:

    p_correct = base_rate + learning_rate*log(trial),

where `trial` can take on the values 1, 2, 3, ..., 200, `learning_rate` can be any real number between 0 and 1, `base_rate` equals 1/4 (i.e., 1 over the number of categories), and `p_correct` cannot exceed 1. Write a program that lets you explore the effects of `learning_rate` on number of trials to criterion. You can set the criterion to whatever value(s) you choose.

6. Input-Output

This chapter covers the following topics:

The commands that are introduced and the sections in which they are premiered are as follows:

`'`	(6.2)
`' '`	(6.2)
`disp`	(6.2)
`input`	(6.2)
`pause`	(6.3)
`format`	(6.5)
`format bank`	(6.5)
`format long`	(6.5)
`format long g`	(6.5)
`format rat`	(6.5)
`format short`	(6.5)
`format short g`	(6.5)
`%%`	(6.6)
`' '`	(6.6)
`%d`	(6.6)
`%e`	(6.6)
`%f`	(6.6)
`\n`	(6.6)
`%s`	(6.6)
`sprintf`	(6.6)

`'s'`	(6.6)
`%s`	(6.6)
`int2str`	(6.7)
`num2str`	(6.7)
`strcat`	(6.7)
`strcmp`	(6.8)
`upper`	(6.8)
`eval`	(6.9)
`genvar`	(6.9)
`fprintf`	(6.10)
`dlmwrite`	(6.11)
`fclose`	(6.11)
`fopen`	(6.11)
`cd`	(6.12)
`dir`	(6.12)
`pwd`	(6.12)
`load`	(6.13)
`xlsread`	(6.14)
`xlswrite`	(6.14)
`exist`	(6.15)
`fgetl`	(6.16)
`fread`	(6.16)
`fseek`	(6.16)
`fwrite`	(6.16)
`iofun`	(6.16)
`textread`	(6.16)

6.1 Copying and Pasting Data by Hand

In all the examples presented so far, matrices have been generated with little control of their format, either for input or for output. In addition, matrices have been output only to the MATLAB command window. Clearly, it would be desirable to have more control of input and output, especially for large data sets. This chapter covers ways of doing this.

One way of getting data into a program is to copy it from another source such as Microsoft Word. A method that can be used for this purpose is to create a program in the M-File Editor, leaving space between the opening and closing brackets of the matrix and then pasting text between those brackets. Here is an example of code that can be created prior to pasting.

Code 6.1.1

```
my_data = [
          ]
```

Output 6.1.1

```
my_data =
     [ ]
```

Having written this code, you can paste text into it. In this case, a 2×4 matrix is pasted in, consisting of the numbers 1 through 4 in the first row and the numbers 5 through 8 in the second row.

Code 6.1.2

```
my_data = [
1 2 3 4
5 6 7 8

          ]
```

Output 6.1.2

```
my_data =
     1    2    3    4
     5    6    7    8
```

One reason for considering this example is to show that the closing bracket for a matrix does not have to be on the same line as the opening bracket, although the opening bracket does have to be on the same line as the equal sign (=).

A word of caution about copying and pasting is that it is safer to paste simple text than formatted text into .m-files. For example, copying several cells of data from an Excel spread sheet can yield unexpected consequences. Likewise, nicely formatted data from Word may make a mess when pasted into MATLAB. If you are going to paste data into a .m file, save the data first as simple text.

Copying and pasting can also be used to transfer the output of a MATLAB program to another file, such as a Word document. After generating a matrix with MATLAB, typically by omitting a semicolon after its name in a MATLAB script, you can select the output from MATLAB's command window, copy it, and paste it elsewhere. Other, more powerful and reliable methods are covered later in this chapter. Copying and pasting by hand can be done in a pinch, but in general is not advisable.

6.2   Getting Input From a User and Displaying the Result

Copying and pasting by hand may be satisfactory for small data sets, but performing these manual operations is generally unsatisfactory for larger data sets.

How else can data be entered into MATLAB? One context in which this question can be addressed is a situation commonly encountered in behavioral science—gathering data interactively, for example, at a bank ATM machine. Suppose you want someone to input data to the computer. The challenge is to design an interactive mode of communication that ensures that the data come in both as you wish and as the user wishes (provided the user is being cooperative).

A function that is very useful in this context is `input`. `input` takes a literal string rather than a number as its argument. In the example that follows, the literal string is, 'What is your favorite number?' When MATLAB encounters the input command, it awaits a signal that the enter or return key has been pressed, at which point it displays the literal string provided as the argument. Notice that apostrophes (' ') surround the text to mark it as a string. Putting a space between the question mark and the final apostrophe leaves a space between the question mark and the user's typed response. The output appears in the command window.

Code 6.2.1

```
favorite = input('What is your favorite number?')
```

Output 6.2.1

```
What is your favorite number?
```

If the user types '3', here is what appears in the command window.

Output 6.2.1a

```
What is your favorite number? 3
favorite =
     3
```

When using input, it is important to "idiot-proof" the interaction. The term "idiot proofing" conveys the idea that users—even well-intentioned, perfectly intelligent ones—may sometimes do unexpected things, such as hitting keys that generate bad data. Consider the following situation.

Code 6.2.2

```
favorite = input('What is your favorite number between 2
and 7?')
```

If the user accidentally types an alphabetic character such as p rather than a number, MATLAB sends an error message because only a number is acceptable in this particular context.

Output 6.2.2

```
??? Undefined function or variable 'p'.
```

Even if the user types a number, there is no guarantee that it will be useful. For example, if the user types a number outside the range of 2 to 7, you are stuck with that value, which may be inconvenient later.

A strategy for idiot-proofing the interaction is to exploit the `while` ... `end` loop (see Chapter 5), as illustrated below. Here the user is asked for his or her favorite number as long as the value of `favorite` is less than 2 or greater than 7. A `while` loop is used for this purpose, and to make sure the `while` loop is entered, `favorite` is initialized to a value less than 2 or greater than 7. A convenient value to use for this purpose is −`inf`.

Code 6.2.3

```
favorite = −inf;
while (favorite < 2) | (favorite > 7)
 favorite = …
       input('What is your favorite number between 2 and 7?')
end
```

Output 6.2.3

```
What is your favorite number between 2 and 7? 88
favorite =
    88
What is your favorite number between 2 and 7? 0
favorite =
    0
What is your favorite number between 2 and 7? 3
favorite =
    3
```

As shown above, the user eventually figures out that there is a problem with his or her answer. However, not all users are as patient or as diligent as one hopes. Consequently, it may help to provide more polite or informative prompts, as illustrated below, where another helpful command, `disp`, is used to display a message in the command window.

Code 6.2.4

```
favorite = −inf;
while (favorite < 2) | (favorite > 7)
    favorite = …
       input('What is your favorite number between 2 and 7? ')
    if (favorite < 2) | (favorite > 7)
      disp('Sorry, is that really the input you intended?')
    end
end
disp(favorite)
```

6.3   Pausing

Sometimes you can help users feel a little less harried by slowing things down. Here the `pause` command is handy. The following code shows how the `pause` command is used.

The program first uses `disp` to show the message to which the user should respond. Then the computer is told to `pause` until a key (any key) is struck.

Code 6.3.1

```
disp('Hit return to go on.')
pause
```

If the program had said `pause(2)`, the computer would have paused for two seconds before going on to the next programmed event, not needing input from the user. Non-integer value arguments of `pause`, such as `pause(2.5)`, are permissible, but the timing is not very reliable. More precise timing can be achieved with PsychToolbox or COGENT (see Section 14.3).

6.4   Recording Reaction Times and Other Delays With `tic … toc`

A favorite measure of behavioral scientists is reaction time, the time for a response after some stimulus. Reaction time provides an index of decision-making. The longer the reaction time, the longer the component processes that led to it, all else being equal.

MATLAB provides a way of recording reaction times. The commands that are needed are called, appropriately enough, `tic` and `toc` (see Section 5.5). The `tic` command causes MATLAB to note the time when the `tic` command is issued. The `toc` command causes MATLAB to note the time when the `toc` command is issued relative to `tic`. It is possible to measure reaction time by having people interact with the computer between `tic` and `toc`, as illustrated below.

Code 6.4.1

```
commandwindow
tic
favorite = input('What is your favorite number?')
RT = toc
```

Output 6.4.1

```
RT =
 2.0830
```

The value of `toc` (in this case, the value of the variable called RT) is expressed in seconds. Note, however, that the speed of your computer can affect the actual value of `toc` in ways that can be difficult to assess. PsychToolbox and COGENT afford more precise timing if such precision is desired (Section 14.3). However, for some purposes, `tic … toc` may be sufficient—for example, if you are only interested in effect sizes that are very large relative to the range of differences among computers. As long as you report in full how your data were collected, others can not only replicate your findings; they can also apply whatever degree of skepticism to your measures your report invites (wittingly or unwittingly on your part).

6.5   Formatting Numbers for Screen Outputs

When data are collected either by copying and pasting or by generating values through calculations and contingencies, you can achieve some control of the form of the output by using the `format` command. By typing `help format` at the MATLAB command line or by reading about `format` in MATLAB's other Help sources, you can learn about the options associated with the `format` command. Here are a few of them. You can best appreciate what each type of format does by looking at Output 6.5.1.

Code 6.5.1

```
t = [0:.1:1]';
format bank
bank_format_t = t

format rat
rational_format_t = t

format short
short_format_t = t

format short g
short_g_format_t = t

format long
long_format_t = t

format long g
long_g_format_t = t

format % return format to standard default
standard_format_t
```

Output 6.5.1

```
bank_format_t =
      0
   0.10
   0.20
   0.30
   0.40
   0.50
   0.60
   0.70
   0.80
   0.90
   1.00
```

```
rational_format_t =
       0
     1/10
      1/5
     3/10
      2/5
      1/2
      3/5
     7/10
      4/5
     9/10
       1

short_format_t =
       0
  0.1000
  0.2000
  0.3000
  0.4000
  0.5000
  0.6000
  0.7000
  0.8000
  0.9000
  1.0000

short_g_format_t =
       0
     0.1
     0.2
     0.3
     0.4
     0.5
     0.6
     0.7
     0.8
     0.9
       1

long_format_t =
                 0
  0.10000000000000
  0.20000000000000
  0.30000000000000
  0.40000000000000
  0.50000000000000
  0.60000000000000
```

```
0.70000000000000
0.80000000000000
0.90000000000000
1.00000000000000

long_g_format_t =
        0
      0.1
      0.2
      0.3
      0.5
      0.6
      0.7
      0.8
      0.9
        1

standard_format_t =
         0
    0.1000
    0.2000
    0.3000
    0.4000
    0.5000
    0.6000
    0.7000
    0.8000
    0.9000
    1.0000
```

6.6   Assigning Arrays of Literal Characters (Strings) to Variables

In the earlier examples of asking a user for his or her favorite number (Code 6.21), the displayed text was surrounded with apostrophes. These characters delimited an array of literal characters, also known as a `string`. MATLAB can be prompted to accept strings as input. In the code that follows, we indicate that a string should be accepted as input. To achieve this, we add a comma and 's' after 'What is your name?'

Code 6.6.1

```
name = input('What is your name? ','s');
```

Output 6.6.1

```
What is your name? David
```

It would be nice to reply to the user by name, but how can you pre-program this action without knowing what the user's name will be? `sprintf` is useful for this purpose. `sprintf`—short for *string print format*—lets you assign data to a string variable. This is illustrated below, where we tell MATLAB to print 'Hello' along with the string variable that follows. Notice that the percent sign is used as a kind of comment here. The percent sign tells MATLAB that the character following it is not part of the string itself. The period (`.`) after `%s` indicates that a period should appear after the string.

Code 6.6.2

```
sprintf('Hello, %s.', name)
```

Output 6.6.2

```
ans =
Hello, David.
```

`%s` is not the only command that can be used with `sprintf`. Other commands of this type are useful as well:

`%d`   indicates that an upcoming variable will be an integer
`%e`   indicates that an upcoming variable will be in scientific notation (e.g., 6.5e6 = 6.5×10^6 = 6.5 million).
`%f`   indicates that an upcoming variable will be a floating point (or decimal) number,

Examples follow.

Code 6.6.3

```
piVal = sprintf('The value of %s is %f', 'pi', pi)
```

Output 6.6.3

```
piVal =
```

```
The value of pi is 3.141593
```

Code 6.6.4

```
int_vs_float = …
    sprintf('Here is the same number printed as …
    an integer %d and as a float %f', 3, 3)
```

Output 6.6.4

```
int_vs_float =
```

```
Here is the same number printed as an integer 3, and as a
float 3.000000
```

There are some other commands worth knowing about:. ' \n ' indicates that a return should be included in a string.

Code 6.6.5

```
twoLines = sprintf('two\nlines')
```

Output 6.6.5

```
twoLines =

two
lines
```

' %% ' indicates that a percent sign (%) should be included in a string.

Code 6.6.6

```
percent = sprintf('Give 100%%')
```

Output 6.6.6

```
percent =

Give 100%
```

' ' indicates that an apostrophe should be included in a string. The output listed below is the answer I provided.

Code 6.6.7

```
name = input('What's your name? ','s');
```

Output 6.6.7

```
What's your name? David
```

A final word about `sprintf` is that the presence of "print" within the word "sprintf" can be misleading. When you use the `sprintf` command, you are not actually printing in a physical sense. Rather, you are assigning data in string format (a sequence of literal, alpha-numeric characters) to a variable.

A further indication that `sprintf` is not a command to physically print a variable is that in the examples above, each line of code that included the `sprintf` command lacked a semicolon at the end of the line. The only property of the foregoing code that allowed the values to be displayed was that semicolons were omitted from the ends of the lines. If you *include* a semicolon at the end of a line that uses `sprintf`, MATLAB takes no observable action, though you can subsequently request the value of the variable to satisfy yourself that the string variable was in fact assigned a value.

Code 6.6.8

```
s = sprintf('ssss');
```

Output 6.6.8

Code 6.6.9

```
s
```

Output 6.6.9

```
s =
ssss
```

6.7 Converting Numbers to Strings, and Concatenating Strings

Sometimes you need to convert numbers to strings, and sometimes you need to concatenate strings. Here is an example of a situation where these two needs arise.

Code 6.7.1

```
f = 7;
disp('Your favorite number is ' f);
```

Output 6.7.1

```
??? Error: File: Number_To_String_01.m Line: 4 Column: 31
Missing MATLAB operator.
```

Why did MATLAB return an error message? The reason is that disp requires a single matrix, consisting of one row of values, all of which need to be of one type, either numbers or literal characters. You can address this problem as follows.

Code 6.7.2

```
f = 7;
disp(['Your favorite number is ' int2str(f)]);
```

Output 6.7.2

```
Your favorite number is 7
```

In Code 6.7.2, the `int2str` command was used to convert an integer (7) to a string. The two strings of interest, `'Your favorite number is'` and `int2str(f)`, were also concatenated into one matrix by listing them within brackets.

It is also possible to convert numbers to strings using the `num2str` command. This preserves the value to the right of the decimal point if one is present.

Another way to concatenate strings is to use the `strcat` command. `strcat` gets rid of trailing spaces:

Code 6.7.3

```
f = 7.2;
disp(strcat('Your favorite number is', num2str(f)))
```

Output 6.7.3

```
Your favorite number is7.2
```

6.8   Comparing Strings

MATLAB provides a way of comparing strings. This can be useful in many contexts, such as deciding whether received input matches required input (e.g., Does the security ID that a user inputs match one in the records?). The following examples show how strings can be compared using the `strcmp` command. Note that outputs of 1 and 0 denote true (the strings match) and false (the strings do not match), respectively. In computer science generally, 1 means true and 0 means false.

Code 6.8.1

```
match_of_aba_and_aba = strcmp('aba','aba')

match_of_aba_and_abc = strcmp('aba','abc')

match_of_aba_and_Aba = strcmp('aba','Aba'=)

match_of_lower_aba_and_lower_Aba = ...
strcmp(lower('aba'),lower('Aba'))

match_of_upper_aba_and_upper_Aba = ...
strcmp(upper('aba'),upper('Aba'))
```

Output 6.8.1

```
match_of_aba_and_aba =
     1

match_of_aba_and_abc =
     0

match_of_aba_and_Aba =
     0

match_of_lower_aba_and_lower_Aba =
     1

match_of_upper_aba_and_upper_Aba =
     1
```

Note that in the third case, which compared `'aba'` and `'Aba'`, the match of the two strings being compared was assigned a score of 0 (mismatch) rather than a score of 1 (match) because at least one pair of characters in corresponding positions did not match. If you don't happen to care about lowercase versus uppercase letters, you can add `lower` or `upper` to the string comparison, as in the fourth and fifth lines of Code 6.8.1.

There are other string-comparison commands in MATLAB. To learn more about them, type `help strcmp` at the command line prompt.

6.9   Evaluating Strings and Generating Numbered Variables on the Fly

MATLAB provides a way of turning strings into executable commands. It does so with the `eval` command. In some instances, `eval` is not terribly useful, as in Code 6.9.1, which shows the syntax for `eval` just to set the stage for the more useful applications to come. As shown in Code 6.9.1, `eval` carries out instructions enclosed in quote marks.

Code 6.9.1

```
t = eval('1 + 4')
```

Output 6.9.1

```
t =
     5
```

Notwithstanding the triviality of the above example, `eval` can serve a useful purpose. Suppose you want to have matrices called `M1`, `M2`, `M3`, and so on. You can define these matrices by hand like this:

Code 6.9.2

```
M1 = [ ];
M2 = [ ];
M3 = [ ];
```

However, it becomes tedious to do this for very long, as in adding M4, M5, and so on, all the way up to M1028, for example. There is a way to solve this problem, using eval (as well as num2str, introduced in Section 6.6). Code 6.9.3 shows how to create M1 through M1028 and check the results by asking for the value of one of the matrices. Be forewarned that the semicolon at the end of the eval statement does not prevent screen output of the individual values.

Code 6.9.3

```
for i = 1:1028
    eval(['M' num2str(i)' = num2str(i*2)']);
end
M18
```

Output 6.9.3

```
M18 =
    36
```

Here is another example using a handy function that MATLAB provides, called genvarname. As its name implies, genvarname lets you generate variable names on the fly. Using genvarname in conjunction with eval lets you assign values to the generated variable. The following program shows how to generate a variable name and then later retrieve a value associated with that variable name.

Code 6.9.4

```
for k = 1:5
    v = genvarname('variable_name_', who);
    eval([v ' = [k*2 k*3 k*4]']);
end
% print the value of variable_name_2
j = 2;
eval(['variable_name_' num2str(j)])
```

Output 6.9.4

```
variable_name_ =
     2    3    4

variable_name_1 =
     4    6    8

variable_name_2 =
     6    9   12

variable_name_3 =
     8   12   16

variable_name_4 =
    10   15   20

variable_name_2 =
     6    9   12
```

For more information about `genvarname` and `eval`, use MATLAB help.

6.10 Controlling File Print Formats

We turn now to one of the most useful commands in MATLAB, `fprintf`, short for *file print format.* As its name suggests, `fprintf` lets you tailor the way your data are printed.

Before showing examples of the `fprintf` command, it is useful to note that the special characters mentioned above in connection with `sprintf` also work with `fprintf`. For review purposes, those special characters are as follows:

%d   indicates that an upcoming variable will be an integer

%e   indicates that an upcoming variable will be in scientific notation
      (e.g., 6.5e6 = 6.5 × 10^6 = 6.5 million).

%f   indicates that an upcoming variable will be a floating point (or decimal)
      number,

%s   indicates that an upcoming variable will be a string

'\n' indicates that a return should be included in a string.

Some examples that use `fprintf` follow.

Code 6.10.1

```
fprintf('%s','Matlab can be fun.');
```

Output 6.10.1

```
Matlab can be fun.
```

Next, we print the matrix `[1:10]` first as integers (using `%d`), then in scientific notation (using `%e`), and finally in floating point notation (using `%f`). We print a return after each line. If we don't tell MATLAB to print the returns, it will not do so.

Code 6.10.2

```
fprintf('%d',[1:10])
fprintf('\n')
fprintf('%e',[1:10])
fprintf('\n')
fprintf('%f',[1:10])
fprintf('\n')
```

Output 6.10.2

```
12345678910
1.000000e+0002.000000e+0003.000000e+0004.000000e+0005.000
000e+0006.000000e+0007.000000e+0008.000000e+0009.000000e+
0001.000000e+001
1.0000002.0000003.0000004.0000005.0000006.0000007.0000008
.0000009.00000010.000000
```

Output 6.10.2 is not especially welcoming. It would be nice to have even greater control of the output. The following example shows how to print the same matrix, `[1:10]`, specifying six columns for each value and treating each value as a floating point number. The notation in quotes means, "Allocate six columns per number with two places to the right of the decimal point, using floating-point notation."

Code 6.10.3

```
fprintf('%6.2f',[1:10])
```

Output 6.10.3

```
  1.00   2.00   3.00   4.00   5.00   6.00   7.00   8.00   9.00  10.00
```

The next example gives more information about how the formatting of numbers can be controlled. After defining `Pi_matrix` as a 1×10 matrix whose values are spaced linearly from `pi` to `2*pi`, we print the values with no spaces to the right of the decimal point and then with two values to the right of the decimal point.

Code 6.10.4

```
Pi_matrix = linspace(pi,2*pi,10);
fprintf('\n');
fprintf('%6.0f', Pi_matrix);
fprintf('\n');
fprintf('%6.2f', Pi_matrix);
fprintf('\n');
```

Output 6.10.4

```
   3       3    4        4    5        5       5       6       6       6

3.14   3.49 3.84    4.19 4.54   4.89   5.24   5.59   5.93   6.28
```

The actual values of `Pi_matrix` are unaffected by the way they are printed.

Code 6.10.5

```
Pi_matrix
```

Output 6.10.5

```
Pi_matrix =
    3.1416   3.4907   3.8397   4.1888   4.5379   4.8869
    5.2360   5.5851   5.9341   6.2832
```

Just as we can control the formatting of real numbers, it is also possible to control the format of integers. Here we allocate four columns per integer, then five columns per integer, and finally six columns per integer.

Code 6.10.6

```
fprintf('%4d',[1:10]);
fprintf('\n');
fprintf('%5d'=,[1:1]);
fprintf('\n');
fprintf('%6d',[1:10]);
```

Output 6.10.6

```
   1   2   3   4   5   6   7   8   9  10
    1   2   3   4   5   6   7   8   9   10
     1    2    3    4    5    6    7    8    9    10
```

Even if a line containing `fprintf` ends with a semicolon, printing still occurs. By contrast, as seen in the last section, `sprintf` assigns a string to a *variable*. For that reason, when an `sprintf` command is issued, the value of the variable is only printed when a semi-colon is removed from the end of the line.

If different formats need to appear in a single line, those formats must be specified individually so each value can be output as desired. Here is an example in which different formats are generated for each of two lines of output.

Code 6.10.7

```
a = [3.1:5.1];
b = [3:5];
c = a*2;
d = b + 2;

fprintf('%6.2f',a);
fprintf('%4d',b);
fprintf('\n');
fprintf('%6.2f',c);
fprintf('%4d',d);
fprintf('\n');
```

Output 6.10.7

```
3.10    4.10    5.10   3   4   5
6.20    8.20   10.20   5   6   7
```

6.11   Writing Data to Named Files

`fprintf` can include the name of the file to which data are written. There is a default file to which data are written with the `fprintf` command when no file name is given. That default file is the command window's currently active line.

The file to which `fprintf` prints need not be the command window's active line. Instead, or in addition, it can be a file that is named and located as you please.

In the following code we define a file to which data is written. We first issue the `fopen` command. The file to be opened (or created) is named `'mydata'`. This is a text file, and so has the suffix `.txt`. We write text to that file, so it has the `'wt'` after the comma. The file name, `fid`, is the file identifier, which is used in subsequent `fprintf` commands. There is nothing special about the name `fid`. We could just as well have called it `ham_and_eggs`.

Once we have opened `fid`, we can write data to it. There is no harm in also writing the data to the command window to make sure it looks the way we expect. In the program that follows, we write data to `fid` as well as the command window, then we write more data to both locations, and finally we close `fid` using the `fclose` command. Until the file is closed, it is not accessible.

In the code that follows, we open a file called `my_data.txt` to which text will be written, we assign the name `fid` to that opened file name, then after defining a matrix called `rr`, we proceed to print `rr` both to `fid` and to the command window. The output format we desire is the one shown in Output 6.11.1. Note that we issue one print command at a time, first for `fid` and then for the command window. The command window is specified implicitly by omitting an output file name after the opening paragraph mark following `fprintf`. The program ends by closing the opened file.

Code 6.11.1

```
fid = fopen('mydata.txt','wt');
rr = [1.1:5.1];

fprintf(fid,'%6.1f',rr);
fprintf('%6.1f',rr);

fprintf(fid,'\n');
fprintf('\n');

fprintf(fid,'%6.1f',rr+2);
fprintf('%6.1f',rr+2);

fprintf('\n')

fclose(fid);
```

Output 6.11.1

```
1.1   2.1   3.1   4.1   5.1
3.1   4.1   5.1   6.1   7.1
```

There are other ways to write data to named files besides `fprintf`. One is to use `dlmwrite`. Here is an example in which the matrix `data` is saved as tab-delimited text to a file called `my_dlm_data`.

Code 6.11.2

```
data = [78:99];
dlmwrite('my_dlm_data.txt',data,'\t');
```

For more information about `dlmwrite` and for pointers to other methods of writing data to named files, type `help dlmwrite` in the MATLAB command line. Type `help iofun` for a complete list of input and output functions available in MATLAB.

6.12   Checking and Changing the Current Directory

The output listed above appeared in the command window. It would be reassuring to confirm that the data also got into `mydata.txt` as hoped.

There are different ways to check this. One is to list the contents of the current directory where, hopefully, `mydata.txt` will be listed. You can list the contents of the current directory with the `ls` command.

Code 6.12.1

```
ls
```

Output 6.12.1

```
fprintf_to_file_1.m
mydata.txt
```

Happily, `mydata.txt` is there. So too is `fprintf_to_file_1.m`, the program used to create `mydata.txt.`

Another way to list the current directory is with `dir`. Here dir is used along with the * wildcard and the suffix that defines the file type (e.g., `.txt`). Here is code that lists `.m files` in the current directory of the author at the time this chapter was being prepared.

Code 6.12.2

```
dir *.m
```

Output 6.12.2

```
Format_Tester_1.m               Sort_1.m
Format_Tester_2.m               Sort_2.m
Imaginary_Numbers_1.m           Stats_Calculations.m
Matrix_Calclulations_1.m        Switch_Test_Program_2.m
Mixed_format_fprintf_test_1.m   Timer_1.m
Mixed_format_fprintf_test_2.m   fprintf_to_file_1.m
Random_Numbers_1.m
Simple_calc_1.m
Simple_calc_2.m
```

To find out the name of the current directory, you can use the `pwd` command.

Code 6.12.3

```
pwd
```

Output 6.12.3

```
ans =
C:\Lab and Teach\PSU Teaching\Programming Seminar\
  Textbook
```

To change the current directory, you can use the `cd` command. To change to a specific named directory, its full path must be supplied, as in this example.

Code 6.12.4

```
cd(>D:\MATLAB of David\=)
pwd
```

Output 6.12.4

```
ans =

D:\MATLAB of David
```

To access the parent directory of the current directory, you can write

Code 6.12.5

```
cd('. .')
pwd
```

Output 6.12.5

```
ans =

D:\
```

Changing the current directory can be useful for accessing data in different directories or for writing data to different directories.

6.13   Reading Data Saved as Plain Text

How can data be read into a program from an external file? One way is to use the `load` command. The name of the file to be loaded must be enclosed in single quote marks. It is easy to forget to include the single quote marks and then be frustrated by error messages that say no such file exists. Be careful about this.

Code 6.13.1

```
data_from_file = load('mydata.txt')
```

Output 6.13.1

```
data_from_file =
      1.1000    2.1000    3.1000    4.1000    5.1000
      3.1000    4.1000    5.1000    6.1000    7.1000
```

You can also use `load` to read files in plain text format that may have been created with other programs such as Microsoft Word. Be sure to save the files in plain text format if you plan to load them.

6.14   Reading Data From and Writing Data to Excel Spreadsheets

Reading data from Microsoft Excel files is easy in MATLAB, as is writing to such files.

Here is how you can read an Excel spreadsheet called `'data'` into a matrix, `M`.

Code 6.14.1

```
M = xlsread('data.xls');
```

You can also specify a particular worksheet to be read within the Excel document.

Code 6.14.2

```
M = xlsread('data.xls', 'Experiment 2');
```

`xlsread` returns only the numeric portion of the spreadsheet. Non-numeric cells are assigned the value `NaN` (short for Not a Number), and column names are ignored.

Writing data to an Excel spreadsheet is easy. The relevant function is `xlswrite`. In Code 6.14.3 `xlswrite` is used to write `M` to an Excel file called `My_Excel_File`.

Code 6.14.3

```
xlswrite('My_Excel_File', M);
```

6.15   Taking Precautions Against Overwriting Files

You may wish to know if the file you are about to write to already exists so you don't overwrite it. MATLAB's `exist` function can be used for this purpose. Code 6.15.1 shows how MATLAB can be used to test for the existence of a file called `filename` and give a warning if that filename is already taken. Note that the check is only made in the current directory.

Code 6.15.1

```
filename = input('File name: ','s');
if ~exist(filename)
     save('filename','rows','-ASCII'=);
else
     disp(['Error: the file '' ' filename ' '' already
          exists!']);
end
```

Sometimes the suffix for a checked file needs to be added. For example, if `exist(mydata)` fails to yield a warning but you know the file is there, it may be that you need to say `exist(mydata.txt)`. These matters should be checked during program development, before you put your program to full use.

6.16 Learning More About `input` and `output`

MATLAB has more functions for input and output. For reading tabular data that includes text fields, `textread` can extract columns using a pattern-matching syntax similar to that of `fprintf`. If the data set is unstructured, it may be necessary to read each line individually with `fgetl` and to do processing on a line-by-line basis. MATLAB can also deal with binary data, as obtained from scientific instruments, using `fread`, `fwrite`, and `fseek`. It is worth checking the documentation and the MathWorks web site before writing new code that uses these commands. Typing `help iofun` can be informative in this regard since the command provides a portal to all the material that has been covered here, plus more.

Code 6.16.1

```
Help iofun
```

Output 6.16.1

```
File input/output.
File import/export functions.
        dlmread     —  Read delimited text file.
        dlmwrite    —  Write delimited text file.
        load        —  Load workspace from MATLAB (MAT) file.
        importdata  —  Load workspace variables disk file.
        wk1read     —  Read spreadsheet (WK1) file.
        wk1write    —  Write spreadsheet (WK1) file.
        xlsread     —  Read spreadsheet (XLS) file.
```

6.17 Practicing `input–output`

Try your hand at the following exercises, using only the methods introduced so far in this book or information given in the problems themselves.

Problem 6.17.1

Write a program that yields the output shown below. Note that each element of B is the corresponding element in A, squared. Each value appears in the output with seven columns per number and with one place to the right of the decimal point. The output should look like this:

```
A

   1.0    2.0    3.0    4.0    5.0    6.0    7.0    8.0    9.0   10.0
  11.0   12.0   13.0   14.0   15.0   16.0   17.0   18.0   19.0   20.0
  21.0   22.0   23.0   24.0   25.0   26.0   27.0   28.0   29.0   30.0
  31.0   32.0   33.0   34.0   35.0   36.0   37.0   38.0   39.0   40.0
  41.0   42.0   43.0   44.0   45.0   46.0   47.0   48.0   49.0   50.0
  51.0   52.0   53.0   54.0   55.0   56.0   57.0   58.0   59.0   60.0
```

B

1.0	4.0	9.0	16.0	25.0	36.0	49.0	64.0	81.0	100.0
121.0	144.0	169.0	196.0	225.0	256.0	289.0	324.0	361.0	400.0
441.0	484.0	529.0	576.0	625.0	676.0	729.0	784.0	841.0	900.0
961.0	1024.0	1089.0	1156.0	1225.0	1296.0	1369.0	1444.0	1521.0	1600.0
1681.0	1764.0	1849.0	1936.0	2025.0	2116.0	2209.0	2304.0	2401.0	2500.0
2601.0	2704.0	2809.0	2916.0	3025.0	3136.0	3249.0	3364.0	3481.0	3600.0

Problem 6.17.2

Write a program that assigns 20 random integers to x followed by 20 random integers to y. Write the x and y values as integers in a text file you first open with the `fopen` command and later close with the `fclose` command. In the text file, allot four columns per integer. Note that you can assign 20 random integers to a matrix of size 20 × 1 with the command `ceil(10.*rand(20,1)`.

Problem 6.17.3

Write a program that creates an Excel file that serves as the spreadsheet into which data from a behavioral science experiment can be saved. The Excel file should have the following columns in each of 200 rows:

Column 1: subject_number (1 to 200)

Column 2: subject_number_parity (odd, denoted 0, or even, denoted 1)

Column 3: A random value drawn from a normal distribution with mean equal to 0 and standard deviation equal to 1 for odd-numbered subjects, or a random value drawn from a normal distribution with mean equal to 10 and standard deviation equal to 5 for even-numbered subjects.

Column 4: NaN, serving as a placeholder for the response to be given.

Column 5: NaN, serving as a placeholder for the accuracy of the response (correct, denoted 1; or incorrect, denoted 0)

Read the Excel file back into MATLAB to observe the effects of adding NaN to Columns 4 and 5.

Problem 6.17.4

Write a program in which a user is asked for a password. The program should check whether the password is contained in a list of three acceptable passwords, defined as follows:

```
correct_passwords = ['A1B2C3'; 'B2C3A1'; 'C3A1B2']
```

Idiot-proof the program so the user is not rejected prematurely if s/he makes a typing error, but only let the user respond to the input a set number of times (e.g., 4).

Problem 6.17.5

Modify the program from Problem 6.4 so passwords consist of random permutations of the integers 0 through 9 and the matrix of passwords is retrieved from an external file. You will need to create the external file first. Set it up so there are 100 passwords for 100 employees. Later, for an employee to enter the system, the password s/he supplies must be the password associated with his or her employee number, which is 1 through 100.

Two pieces of information will help you solve this fairly difficult problem. One is that you can generate a (100×1) matrix of passwords consisting of six integers per row with the following commands:

```
number_of_employees = 100;
passwords = fix(rand(number_of_employees,1)*1000000);
```

Second, you need to convert the password number entered by the user to a number from a string. You can achieve this conversion with a command that is officially premiered in Chapter 8, str2num. The following code segments are also useful in this program. Note that the if statement need not immediately follow the input statement in your program.

```
password = input('What is your 6 character password?', 's')

if correct_passwords(employee_number,:) — str2num(password)
    == 0
      OK_to_enter = 1;
end
```

7. Data Types

This chapter covers the following topics:

The commands that are introduced and the sections in which they are premiered are as follows:

```
class              (7.1)
double             (7.1)
single             (7.1)

char               (7.2)

{ }                (7.3)
cell2mat           (7.3)

record.field       (7.4)
```

7.1   Identifying Strings, Numbers of Different Types, and Booleans

Previous chapters made extensive use of numbers (including matrices consisting of numbers) and strings (sequences of alphabetic or numeric characters not directly usable in numerical calculations). It turns out that there are different types of numbers in MATLAB as well as other data types.

Consider the following code.

Code 7.1.1:

```
clear all
a = 'a'
b = 1
c = 1.00
d = round(c)
e = single(d)
f = true
g = false
whos
```

Output 7.1.1:

```
a =
      a
b =
      1
c =
      1
d =
      1
e =
      1
f =
      1
g =
      0
```

```
Name    Size        Bytes    Class
a       1x1         2        char array
b       1x1         8        double array
c       1x1         8        double array
d       1x1         8        double array
e       1x1         4        single array
f       1x1         1        logical array
g       1x1         1        logical array
```

```
The grand total equals seven elements using 32 bytes
```

As seen above,

a, which was set to 'a', is an array of type char and uses two bytes of memory;

b, which was set to 1, is an array of type double and uses eight bytes of memory;

c, which was set to 1.00, is an array of type double and also uses eight bytes of memory;

d, which was set to round(c), is an array of type double and again uses eight bytes of memory;

e, which was set to single(c), is an array of type single and uses just four bytes of memory;

f and g, which were set to logical or "Boolean" values (after the British logician George Boole) are each arrays of type logical (i.e., true or false) and each uses just one byte of memory.

These examples show several things. One is that a number, by default, is a double (i.e., a number stored with double value precision, requiring eight bytes of memory). Another is that even when a double is rounded, it takes eight bytes of memory. This is true even if the number is passed through `floor` or `ceil` (see Chapter 4). A third is that a number can be a `single` (i.e., a number stored with single value precision, requiring just four bytes of memory. A fourth is that variables can be assigned to the type known as `logical`, whose possible values are `1`, `true`, `0`, or `false`. `1` and `true` mean the same thing, as do `0` and `false`.

Why is it helpful to know about data types? One reason is that different data types require different amounts of memory. Thus, a variable of type `double` requires more memory than a variable of type `single`. This fact can be very important if your program is memory-intensive (i.e., it uses a great many variables or very large data sets).

It is easy to convert values of one data type to another. The possible conversion commands can be found via `help datatypes`. The output generated by typing `help datatypes` is more complete than what follows, but the material shown next is likely to be most relevant to your immediate needs.

Code 7.1.2:

```
help datatypes
```

Output 7.1.2:

```
Data types and structures.

Data types (classes)
      double   —   Convert to double precision.
      logical  —   Convert numeric values to logical.
      cell     —   Create cell array.
      struct   —   Create or convert to structure array.
      single   —   Convert to single precision.
      uint8    —   Convert to unsigned 8-bit integer.
      uint16   —   Convert to unsigned 16-bit integer.
      uint32   —   Convert to unsigned 32-bit integer.
      uint64   —   Convert to unsigned 64-bit integer.
      int8     —   Convert to signed 8-bit integer.
      int16    —   Convert to signed 16-bit integer.
      int32    —   Convert to signed 32-bit integer.
      int64    —   Convert to signed 64-bit integer.
```

You can learn the data type of a variable by using the `class` function, as in this example.

Code 7.1.3:

```
double_value = 2
class(double_value)
single_value = single(double_value)
class(single_value)
```

Output 7.1.3:

```
double_value =

     2

ans =

double

single_value =

     2

ans =

single
```

7.2   Converting Characters to Numbers and Vice Versa

Special attention is warranted for some items in Output 7.1.2. One is the relation between char and double and equivalently, for present purposes, the relation between char and single. When double or single is applied to a string of characters, the computer's numerical equivalents for the characters are given. Remember that as far as the computer is concerned, all data are ultimately represented as binary digits or "bits," which is short for binary digits. This is true regardless of whether the data are characters, numbers, or, for that matter, images or sounds. Therefore, it should not be surprising that MATLAB provides a way of translating from one data type to another since all data are ultimately expressed as bits.

The code below shows how you can get the numerical equivalents of characters using the double function.

Code 7.2.1

```
de = double('!')
dq = double('Our days are numbered!')
```

Output 7.2.1

```
de =
    33

dq =
Columns 1 through 14
    79 117 114   32 100   97 121 115   32   97 114 101   32 110

Columns 15 through 22
   117 109   98 101 114 101 100   33
```

Whereas `double` gives the numbers associated with characters, `char` gives the characters associated with numbers. The following program shows the character equivalents of the numerical matrices `de` and `dq`.

Code 7.2.2

```
de_lettered = char(de)
dq_lettered = char(dq)
```

Output 7.2.2

```
de_lettered =
!
dq_lettered =
our days are numbered!
```

Converting between characters and numbers can be useful in some situations—for example, when assigning verbal responses to numerical quantities.

7.3   Creating and Accessing Cells

Output 7.1.2 mentions a data type not previously mentioned in this book—the `cell`. Cells allow for mixed arrays.

Here `c` is assigned a mixed array, one whose two rows have different numbers of columns. It should come as no surprise that MATLAB balks at the assignment.

Code 7.3.1

```
clear all
c = [1:2;3:5]
```

Output 7.3.1

```
??? Error using ==> vertcat
All rows in the bracketed expression must have the same
number of columns.
```

When the number of columns or rows of data is not uniform, as in Code 7.3.1, the `cell` data type comes in handy.

To assign variables to a cell, use braces rather than brackets.

Code 7.3.2

```
clear c
c = {1:2;3:5}
```

Output 7.3.2

```
c =
     [1x2 double]
     [1x3 double]
```

MATLAB indicates that c consists of two matrices of type `double`, one of which has size 1 × 2 and the other of which has size 1 × 3.

Although Output 7.3.2 tells you what cell c consists of, it does not tell you what its contents are. One way to access cell data is to use the `cell2mat` command.

Code 7.3.3

```
c1 = cell2mat(c(1))
c2 = cell2mat(c(2))
c2(2:3)
```

Output 7.3.3

```
c1 =
     1   2

c2 =
     3   4   5

ans =
     4   5
```

Another way is to use brackets and parentheses.

Code 7.3.4

```
c = {[ 1 2 3]
     [4 5 6 7]
     ['rats mice']; [' d']
     [['rats mice'] [' d']]
     [1 3]}

c_first_row = c{1,:,:}
c_second_row = c{2,:,:}
c_third_row = c{3,:,:}
c_third_row_again = c{3}

disp('c first row column 1 and second row column 1')
% Assigning this to a variable would cause problems
c{1:2,1}
d = {[1 2] [3 4 5]
     [6 7] [8 9 10]}
```

```
d_first_row_first_column = d{1,1}
d_first_row_first_column_element_1 = d{1,1}(2)
d_second_row_second_column_elements_2_and3 = d{2,2}(2:3)
```

Output 7.3.4

```
c =
     [1x3 double]
     [1x4 double]
     'rats mice'
     ' d'
     'rats mice d'
     [1x2 double]

c_first_row =
     1    2    3

c_second_row =
     4    5    6    7

c_third_row =

rats mice

c_third_row_again =

rats mice

c first row column 1 and second row column 1

ans =
     1    2    3

ans =
     4    5    6    7

d =
     [1x2 double]    [1x3 double]
     [1x2 double]    [1x3 double]

d_first_row_first_column =
     1    2

d_first_row_first_column_element_1 =
     2

d_second_row_second_column_elements_2_and3 =
     9    10
```

As seen in the code and output above, elements of cells can be addressed in the same way that elements of matrices can be addressed, by listing the relevant row(s) and column(s). When particular elements within a row and column submatrix are addressed, the indices for those elements can be specified in parentheses after the closing bracket, as in the last two lines of Code 7.3.3.

Cells are particularly useful for arrays that combine strings and numbers. This point is illustrated in the next program, where we create a cell called `Names_and_Numbers` which not only has names and numbers, but also has names and numbers of different lengths. To access individual values within `Names_and_Numbers`, we use `cell2mat`. Note that in Code 7.3.5, the opening brace must appear on the same line as = . As seen in Output 7.3.5, `cell2mat` not only converts numbers within cells to doubles; it also converts strings within cells to characters.

Code 7.3.5

```
Names_and_Numbers = {
'Bob' 90
'Jane' 100
}
cell2mat(Names_and_Numbers(1,1))
cell2mat(Names_and_Numbers(1,2))
```

Output 7.3.5

```
Names_and_Numbers =
      'Bob'  [ 90]
      'Jane' [100]
ans =
      Bob
ans =
      90
```

Having obtained the contents of the cell, we can make use of them as we do other kinds of data.

7.4   Creating and Accessing Structures

Data sets often have hierarchical structure. For example, a house has a kitchen of some area, a living room of some area, a dining room of some area, and so on. Another house has the same room types, each with the same or different areas. Because areas characterize rooms of the same type in different houses, it can be useful to represent data about room areas in a way that reflects this structural feature. The structure, or MATLAB's `struct`, serves this purpose.

Code 7.4.1 presents a way of representing data about kitchens, dining rooms, and living rooms of three houses, treating the data as structures rather than as ordinary matrices. The structure as a whole consists of several *records*, each of which has an optional index—(1), (2), or (3) in this example—and a *field* following the period.

After assigning areas to the kitchen, dining room, and living room of each house, we query the system about the `house` structure as a whole, about `house(3)` in particular, about the `kitchen` of Houses 2 and 3, and about the `living_room` of all the houses. After that, we perform calculations with the fields, in this case by summing the areas of the kitchens.

Code 7.4.1

```
house(1).kitchen = 30^2;
house(1).dining_room = 40^2;
house(1).living_room = 50^2;

house(2).kitchen = 40^2;
house(2).dining_room = 50^2;
house(2).living_room = 60^2;

house(3).kitchen = 50^2;
house(3).dining_room = 60^2;
house(3).living_room = 70^2;

house
house(3)
house(2:3).kitchen
house(:).living_room

totalkitchen = 0;
for k=1:3
     totalkitchen = house(k).kitchen + totalkitchen;

end
totalkitchen
```

Output 7.4.1

```
house =
1x3 struct array with fields:
     kitchen
     dining_room
     living_room
ans =
     kitchen:      2500
     dining_room:  3600
     living_room:  4900
ans =
                   1600
```

```
ans  =
                 2500
ans  =
                 2500
ans  =
                 3600
ans  =
                 4900
ans  =
                 5000
```

Exposure to structures helps pave the way for a better understanding of MATLAB's graphics. As seen in Chapter 9 through Chapter 12, figures are stored as structures, with records and fields. Changing a particular property of a figure, such as its position, is achieved by changing a field.

A final remark about structures is that their fields need not be restricted to single values. Although in the previous example, each field (each room) had a single area, a single value in MATLAB is just a matrix of size 1×1. The number of rows and columns of a field can exceed 1. Indeed, if you think about the statement given at the end of the last paragraph, that the position of a figure is a field, you realize that such a field must be larger than 1×1. The reason is that the position of a figure must have at least four values: the smallest x, the largest x, the smallest y, and the largest y.

Here is another example of a program that uses structures. The structure is called subject. It contains data from two subjects. Subject 1 has reaction times (RTs) and errors for three trials in two sessions, whereas subject 2 has RTs and errors for three trials in *three* sessions. The fact that the number of sessions is not the same for the two subjects causes no problems. Nor does the fact that subject(2) has two fields not found in subject(1), namely, debrief and comment. Note finally that the comment field is a string whereas the other fields are numbers. Structures can accommodate such heterogeneity.

Code 7.4.2

```
subject(1).RTs = [
     500   400   350;
     450   375   325
     ];
subject(1).errors = [
     10   8   6;
     4   3   2
     ] ;

subject(2).RTs = [
     600   500   450;
     550   475   425;
     500   425   400
     ];
```

```
subject(2).errors = [
     10   8   6;
     4    3   2
     3    2   1
     ] ;

subject(2).debrief = 1

subject(2).comment = 'That was a really cool experiment!';

subject

for s = 1:2
    subject(s).RTs(:,:)
    subject(s).errors(:,:)
    subject(s).debrief(:,:)
end
```

Output 7.4.2

```
subject =
1x2 struct array with fields:
    RTs
    errors
    debrief
ans =
    500 400 350
    450 375 325
ans =
     10    8    6
      4    3    2
ans =
    [ ]
ans =
    600 500 450
    550 475 425
    500 425 400
ans =
     10    8    6
      4    3    2
      3    2    1
ans =
      1
ans =

That was a really cool experiment!
```

7.5 Practicing Data Types

Try your hand at the following exercises, using only the methods introduced so far in this book or in information given in the problems themselves.

Problem 7.5.1

Code 7.3.4 contained the following three lines.

```
disp('c first row column 1 and second row column 1')
% Assigning this to a variable would cause problems
c{1:2,1}
```

Recalling that

```
c = {[ 1 2 3]
     [4 5 6 7]
     ['rats mice']; [' d']
     [['rats mice'] [' d']]
     [1 3]}
```

What problem arises when c{1:2,1} is assigned to an ordinary variable named, for example, K? How can this problem be solved? After you have found the way to assign the contents of c{1:2,1} to K, write a command that lists the second and third columns of the second row of K.

Problem 7.5.2

Using Code 7.4.2, compute the Pearson product-moment correlation coefficient for the relation between RTs and errors for subject 1 and, separately, for subject 2. Also compute the Pearson product-moment correlation coefficient for the relation between the trial means of the two subjects' RTs and the trial means of the two subjects' errors.

Problem 7.5.3

Create a cell array, C, whose first column contains the numbers 1 through 100 and whose second column contains the character equivalents of the numbers 1 through 100.

Problem 7.5.4

Use fprintf to print the 33rd through 100th rows of C. Display the numbers 1 through 100 as integers, place a space between each integer and its character equivalent, and place a return after each character.

Problem 7.5.5

Write a program to administer a computerized questionnaire on a topic of interest to you. Use a structure data type and allow participants to answer with whole sentences or phrases for at least some items. Save the data in an external file. Record the time to answer each question.

8.   Modules and Functions

This chapter covers the following topics:

8.1   Taking a top-down approach to programming by using modules
8.2   Writing and using general-purpose functions
8.3   Getting multiple outputs from functions
8.4   Giving multiple inputs to functions
8.5   Creating subfunctions
8.6   Calling functions properly
8.7   Drawing on previously defined functions versus creating your own
8.8   Practicing modules and functions

The new commands that are introduced and the sections in which they are premiered are as follows:

```
ctrl-d          (8.1)

function        (8.2)
```

8.1   Taking a Top-Down Approach to Programming by Using Modules

All the programs presented so far are relatively small because they merely illustrate different approaches to larger programming needs. As programs grow, they tend to become more complex. With greater length and complexity, programs can become conceptual labyrinths in which one may feel like a rat lost in a maze.

The purpose of this chapter is to prevent such "rats' nests." Expressed more positively, this chapter aims to help you create code that is clear and flexible. Code can be clear if it is designed in a modular fashion (i.e., broken into meaningful sub-programs). It can be flexible if it is equipped with general-purpose functions. The next section focuses on functions. The present section focuses on modules, a term I use to refer to stand-alone programs that perform one or a very small number of instructions.

To illustrate the value of modular programming, consider the following example. You want to create a program for selecting students for admission to a college. Here is code that illustrates how the selection procedure might work. Rest assured that this program is not actually being used at any institution of higher education, at least as far as I know. The code is less transparent than it might be. I therefore encourage you just to skim it. A simpler, modular, version follows.

Code 8.1.1:

```
% College_Admissions_04

% Assuming that SATs and GPAs are related to IQs,
% this program generates dummy data for SATs, GPAs,
% Extra-curriculars (EC), and distance (Dist) from the
% college, giving larger scores to greater distance from
% the college (for geographical diversity).
% The SATS and GPAs are summed, each of the student's
% three new scores (Acad, EC, and Dist) are normed, and
% then the min required score for admission is gradually
% increased until the number admitted no longer exceeds
% max_admits_allowed.

% Clear variables, clear and open the commandwindow
clear all
clc
commandwindow

% Set constants
applications = 30;
max_admits_allowed = 10;

IQmean = 110;
IQsd = 20;
SATQsd = 10;
SATVsd = 10;
ECsd = 10;
GPAsd = 10;

Required_Score_Increase = .05;

% Generate dummy scores to test the program
for a = 1:applications
    IQ(a) = IQmean + abs(randn)*IQsd;
    SATQ(a) = IQ(a) + abs(randn)*SATQsd;
    SATV(a) = IQ(a) + abs(randn)*SATVsd;
    GPA(a) = IQ(a) + abs(randn)*GPAsd;
    Acad(a) = SATQ(a) + SATV(a) + GPA(a);
    EC(a) = abs(randn)*ECsd;
    Dist(a) = abs(randn);
end
```

```
% Normalize the scores
Acad = (Acad - min(Acad)) ./ (max(Acad)-min(Acad));
EC = (EC -min(EC)) ./(max(EC)-min(EC));
Dist = (Dist - min(Dist)) ./(max(Dist)-min(Dist));

% Create a Scores matrix, including, in the final column,
% each student's total score
Scores = [Acad' EC' Dist'];
Total_Scores = sum(Scores');
Scores = [Scores Total_Scores'];

% Increase min_Required_Score until
% Students_Accepted <= max_admits_allowed
min_Required_Score = min(Scores(:,end));
Students_Accepted = inf; % To ensure entering while

while Students_Accepted > max_admits_allowed
    min_Required_Score = min_Required_Score + …
        Required_Score_Increase;
    Students_Accepted = 0;
    for a = 1:applications
        Acceptance(a) = 0;
        if Scores(a,end) > min_Required_Score
            Acceptance(a) = 1;
            Students_Accepted = Students_Accepted + 1;
        end
    end
end

% Display the results
disp('Student Number, Academics, EC, Distance, …
    Total Score, Acceptance')
disp(' ')
Scores_And_Acceptances = [Scores Acceptance'];
[r,c] = size(Scores_And_Acceptances);
for i = 1:r
    fprintf('%4d',i)
    fprintf('%6.2f',Scores_And_Acceptances(i,1:end-1))
    fprintf('%4d',Scores_And_Acceptances(i,end))
    fprintf('\r')
end
Students_Accepted
min_Required_Score
```

Output 8.1.1:

```
Student Number, Academics, EC, Distance, Total Score,
Acceptance
        1   0.53    0.60    0.38    1.51    1
        2   0.26    0.19    0.93    1.38    1
        3   0.65    0.00    0.44    1.08    0
        4   1.00    0.38    0.67    2.05    1
        5   0.17    0.92    0.89    1.98    1
        6   0.35    0.07    0.51    0.93    0
        7   0.02    0.28    0.15    0.44    0
        8   0.35    0.03    0.20    0.57    0
        9   0.52    0.44    0.24    1.20    0
       10   0.33    0.85    0.36    1.54    1
       11   0.29    0.21    0.17    0.67    0
       12   0.54    0.27    0.53    1.33    1
       13   0.15    0.21    0.00    0.36    0
       14   0.14    0.04    0.17    0.35    0
       15   0.21    0.18    0.82    1.21    0
       16   0.18    0.50    0.24    0.92    0
       17   0.22    0.29    0.41    0.92    0
       18   0.06    0.37    0.01    0.44    0
       19   0.19    0.02    0.08    0.29    0
       20   0.37    0.18    0.10    0.65    0
       21   0.26    0.69    0.11    1.06    0
       22   0.79    1.00    0.48    2.27    1
       23   0.15    0.97    0.62    1.74    1
       24   0.26    0.68    0.05    0.99    0
       25   0.25    0.10    0.26    0.62    0
       26   0.00    0.69    0.22    0.91    0
       27   0.21    0.13    0.32    0.66    0
       28   0.66    0.63    0.26    1.55    1
       29   0.34    0.20    1.00    1.54    1
       30   0.42    0.14    0.34    0.91    0

Students_Accepted =
     10

min_Required_Score =
      1.2392
```

Code 8.1.1 is hard to follow because it is lengthy and intricate. The program was written with an outline in mind, but the outline is not readily apparent in the code.

The following code shows how the foregoing material can be organized as a series of distinct programs or modules. (Note that the term "module" has no special technical meaning in MATLAB.) Organizing the code in a modular fashion reflects a top-down approach to programming rather than a completely bottom-up approach. It is useful to take a top-down approach as well as a bottom-up approach to programming because the top-down approach helps you focus on the large-scale organization of your program. An entirely bottom-up approach tends to keep you focused on the syntax of individual lines of code. Generating code in a top-down fashion becomes more natural as the lower-level details become more automatic. This is why modules and functions are introduced at this point in the book rather than earlier.

In the material that follows, Code 8.1.1 is broken down into modules. Code 8.1.2 is the main program, Code 8.1.3 is the first program called by the main program, Code 8.1.4 is the second program called by the main program, and so on. Notice that each called program indicates, via a comment, which program called it (the main program in this case). Commented references to calling programs help you keep track of the lineage of your programs.

Code 8.1.2:

```
% College_Admissions_Main.m
Clear_Start;
Set_Constants;
Generate_Dummy_Scores;
Normalize_Scores;
Create_Scores_Matrix;
Select_Students;
Display_Results;
```

Code 8.1.3:

```
% Clear_Start.m

% Called by College_Admissions_Main.m

clear all
clc
commandwindow
```

Code 8.1.4:

```
% Set_Constants.m

% Called by College_Admissions_Main.m

applications = 30;
max_admits_allowed = 10;

IQmean = 110;
IQsd = 20;
SATQsd = 10;
SATVsd = 10;
ECsd = 10;
GPAsd = 10;
Required_Score_Increase = .05;
```

Code 8.1.5:

```
% Generate_Dummy_Scores.m

% Called by College_Admissions_Main.m

for a = 1:applications

    IQ(a) = IQmean + abs(randn)*IQsd;
    SATQ(a) = IQ(a) + abs(randn)*SATQsd;
    SATV(a) = IQ(a) + abs(randn)*SATVsd;
    GPA(a) = IQ(a) + abs(randn)*GPAsd;

    Acad(a) = SATQ(a) + SATV(a) + GPA(a);

    EC(a) = abs(randn)*ECsd;
    Dist(a) = abs(randn);

end
```

Code 8.1.6:

```
% Normalize_Scores.m

% Called by College_Admissions_Main.m

Acad = (Acad - min(Acad)) ./ (max(Acad)-min(Acad));
EC = (EC -min(EC)) ./(max(EC)-min(EC));
Dist = (Dist - min(Dist)) ./(max(Dist)-min(Dist));
```

Code 8.1.7:

```
% Create_Scores_Matrix.m

% Called by College_Admissions_Main.m

% Create a Scores matrix, including, in final column,
% each student's total score
Scores = [Acad' EC' Dist'];
Total_Scores = sum(Scores');
Scores = [Scores Total_Scores'];
```

Code 8.1.8:

```
% Select_Students.m

% Called by College_Admissions_Main.m

% Increase min_Required_Score until
% Students_Accepted <= max_admits_allowed
min_Required_Score = min(Scores(:,end));
Students_Accepted = inf; %To ensure entering while loop
while Students_Accepted > max_admits_allowed
    min_Required_Score = min_Required_Score + …
        Required_Score_Increase;
```

```
       Students_Accepted = 0
       for a = 1:applications
           Acceptance(a) = 0;
           if Scores(a,end) > min_Required_Score
               Acceptance(a) = 1;
               Students_Accepted = Students_Accepted + 1;
           end
       end
end
```

Code 8.1.9:

```
% Display_Results.m

% Called by College_Admissions_Main.m
disp('Student Number, Academics, EC, Distance, …
Total Score, Acceptance')
disp(' ')
Scores_And_Acceptances = [Scores Acceptance'];
[r,c] = size(Scores_And_Acceptances);
for i = 1:r
    fprintf('%4d',i)
    fprintf('%6.2f',Scores_And_Acceptances(i,1:end-1))
    fprintf('%4d',Scores_And_Acceptances(i,end))
    fprintf('\r')
end
Students_Accepted
min_Required_Score
```

Of all the programs listed above (Codes 8.1.2 through 8.1.9), only one needs to be run directly by the user: the main program (Code 8.1.2). When that program is run, it calls the programs listed within it. Each of those programs in turn calls other programs listed within them. Note that this is only possible because each program referred to in Codes 8.1.2 through Code 8.1.9 was previously stored as a stand-alone `.m` script (see Chapter 2). The output is the same as before (Output 8.1.1).

One other feature of modular programming that makes the approach appealing is that a simple keystroke sequence lets you jump from one program to another. Hitting `ctrl–d` on a PC or `apple–d` on a Mac when your cursor is on the name of a program that can be called by the program you are looking at brings up that other program, provided it is in the same directory and has been saved with the name you are clicking on.

8.2   Writing and Using General-Purpose Functions

One reason why the programs in Codes 2.1.2 through 2.1.9 work is that they make use of the same variables. Thus, `Generate_Dummy_Scores.m` (Code 8.1.5) makes use of the values created in `Set_Constants.m` (Code 8.1.4), `Normalize_Scores.m` (Code

8.1.6) makes use of the values created in `Generate_Dummy_Scores.m` (Code 8.1.5), and so on. Variables that are available to different, currently active programs are known as *global variables*.

As you might imagine, global variables can be a great convenience. On the other hand, there are times when global variables can be a bit of a nuisance. Those times are when functions are used. What are functions in MATLAB and why do global variables tend to be a nuisance in connection with them? Are functions only nuisances, or do they have some redeeming qualities?

Functions in MATLAB are basically the same as ordinary functions in mathematics. They take inputs and generate outputs. The relation between the input and output of a function in math or in MATLAB is precisely what defines the function, and getting from the input to the output is precisely what the function does. The most important feature of a function is its generality. When a function is used, it generates an output from any arbitrary input, provided the input is acceptable and provided the necessary calculations are well-defined.

You have seen many calls to MATLAB functions in this book. Examples are `mean`, `median`, `disp`, and `double`.

It is useful to recall the syntax for a function call. Consider this simple example:

Code 8.2.1:

```
r = [1:99];
mean_r = mean(r)
```

Output 8.2.1:

```
mean_r =
     50
```

When the `mean` function is called, it computes the arithmetic average of `r`, taking the values of `r` as input for the necessary calculations.

The input to a function is sometimes referred to as the *argument* for the function. When a function is called in MATLAB, it assigns the argument to the function as input. The function then returns output to the calling program.

Here is an example of a new function called `normalize` which we create after realizing that it would be useful to have a general-purpose function to translate the values in any given numerical array to values ranging from 0 to 1, where 0 is assigned to the smallest value, 1 is assigned to the largest value, and values in between are assigned numbers equal to their proportional distance from the minimum as compared to the maximum distance from the minimum (see Code 8.1.6). The reason it is useful to create such a function is that it is inconvenient to have to change the terms in 8.1.6 to some other terms for every possible normalizing problem. Similarly, it is confusing to stick with the terms originally used (e.g., `Acad`) in some other context where `Acad` is not relevant (e.g., amusement park ratings). We want a function that carries out computations on variables with generic names, such as the letter `x`.

There are five keys to creating a function. First, the function must be saved as a `.m` script. Second, the name of the saved `.m` script must be the name of the function itself. Third, within the code itself, the first term of the first executable line (after any comments) must be the word `function`. Fourth, the syntax of the first executable line must be of the form:

```
function output = name_of_function(input)
```

Fifth, the subsequent executable line or lines of code must be the operations that need to be performed.

Here is code for the new function, `normalize`.

Code 8.2.2:

```
% normalize.m
function y = normalize(x)
y = (x - min(x)) ./ (max(x)-min(x));
```

We can check that the new function works.

Code 8.2.3:

```
x = [1:11];
normalized_values = normalize(x)
```

Output 8.2.3:

```
normalized_values =

Columns 1 through 8

      0    0.1000    0.2000    0.3000    0.4000    0.5000
0.6000    0.7000

Columns 9 through 11

   0.8000    0.9000    1.0000
```

Note that in Code 8.2.3, the name of the input array to `normalize` is x. x is also the name of the variable used in `normalize`. Will the function still work if the name of the argument is not the same as the name of the variable used in the function? The following example shows that it will, demonstrating that the function takes the argument supplied to the function (in this next case, the array called a) and assigns it to the array it uses (in this case, x).

Code 8.2.4:

```
clear normalized_values
a = [1:11];
normalized_values = normalize(a)
```

Output 8.2.4:

```
normalized_values =

Columns 1 through 8

     0    0.1000    0.2000    0.3000    0.4000    0.5000
0.6000    0.7000

Columns 9 through 11

   0.8000    0.9000    1.0000
```

What happens if we ask for the value of y, which is the name of the output generated in normalize (see Code 8.2.2.), after normalize has returned its output?

Code 8.2.5:

```
a = [1:11];
normalize(a);
y
```

Output 8.2.5:

```
??? Undefined function or variable 'y'.
```

Surprisingly, we get an error message. MATLAB tells us that y is an undefined function or variable. What did we do wrong?

Nothing. The reason for the message is that variables inside functions are *local* variables, not *global* variables. The designers of MATLAB appreciated that much as one might want to use special, generic terms inside a variety of functions (e.g., x in a function that normalizes, x in a function that returns the mean, and so on), it would be best to keep the variables inside functions restricted to, or "local" to those functions, at least by default.

8.3 Getting Multiple Outputs From Functions

The function normalize generates only one output. However, MATLAB functions can give multiple outputs. Consider this example, a function that calculates a median split (finds values above and below the median) and then normalizes the scores in the lower half separately from the scores in the upper half.

Code 8.3.1:

```
function [ly, uy] = normalize_split(x);
lx = [];
ux = [];
```

```
for j = 1:length(x)
     if x(j) <= median(x)
         lx = [lx x(j)];
     else
         ux = [ux x(j)];
     end
end
uy = (ux - min(ux)) ./ (max(ux)-min(ux));
ly = (lx - min(lx)) ./ (max(lx)-min(lx));
```

We can check that the function works by calling it. In so doing, we must be sure that each of the two outputs, `uy` and `ly`, are mapped to variables available to the calling program. In this case, we refer to the mapped output variables as `lower_normed` and `upper_normed`, respectively.

Code 8.3.2:

```
a = linspace(20,22,10).^3;
[lower_normed, upper_normed] = normalize_split(a)
```

Output 8.3.2:

```
lower_normed =
     0    .2305    .4737    .7301    1.000
upper_normed =
     0    .2327    .4768    .7324    1.000
```

Note that the outputs, like the inputs, can have different names in the function and in the calling program.

8.4   Giving Multiple Inputs to Functions

Calls to functions can have more than one input argument. When multiple arguments are used by a function, they are used in the order in which they are provided (from left to right). It is important to keep this constraint in mind.

Here is an example in which `normalize_split_two_args` takes two arguments rather than one, as in the previous examples. The function does different things depending on the second argument. It normalizes scores above or below the *median* of the input array if the second argument is 0, or it normalizes scores above or below the *mean* of the input array if the second argument is 1. If the second argument is neither 0 nor 1, an error message is displayed.

Code 8.4.1:

```
% normalize_split_two_args.m
function [ly, uy] = normalize_split_two_args(x,i);
lx = [];
ux = [];
if i == 0 % median split
    for j = 1:length(x)
        if x(j) <= median(x)
            lx = [lx x(j)];
        else
            ux = [ux x(j)];
        end
    end
elseif i == 1 % mean split
    for j = 1:length(x)
        if x(j) <= mean(x)
            lx = [lx x(j)];
        else
            ux = [ux x(j)];
        end
    end
else % error feedback
    disp('An error was made in the call to …
    normalize_split');
end

ly. = (lx - min(lx)) ./ (max(lx)- min(lx));
uy = (ux - min(ux)) ./ (max(ux)- min(ux));
```

Calls to `normalize_split_two_args` follow, after which the output is shown.

Code 8.4.2:

```
a = logspace(20,22,10);
[median_based_lower_norm,median_based_upper_norm_mean] = …
    normalize_split_two_args(a,0)
[mean_based_lower_norm,mean_based_upper_norm] = …
    normalize_split_two_args(a,1)
[other_based_lower_norm,other_based_upper_norm_mean] = …
    normalize_split_two_args(a,3)
```

Output 8.4.2:

```
median_based_lower_norm =
     0    0.0991   0.2644   0.5401   1.0000
median_based_upper_norm_mean =
     0    0.0991   0.2644   0.5401   1.0000
mean_based_lower_norm =
     0    0.0325   0.0868   0.1773   0.3282   0.5800   1.0000
mean_based_upper_norm =
     0    0.3748   1.0000
```

An error was made in the call to normalize_split

```
other_based_lower_norm =
    [ ]
other_based_upper_norm_mean =
    [ ]
```

8.5   Creating Subfunctions

You can call a function within a function. For example, the functions `min` and `max` were called in Code 8.2.2. You can also call a function that is listed along with the function that calls it. Such an internal, subordinate, function is called a *subfunction*.

Here is a function that contains a subfunction. The function, called `mean_and_trimmed_mean`, returns the mean of an array as well as the mean of the trimmed array. The array is trimmed via the subfunction `trimmed`.

Code 8.5.1:

```
function [y,ty] = mean_and_trimmed_mean(x)

y = mean(x);
ty = mean(trimmed(x));
function yy = trimmed(x)

yy = [x(1):x(end-1)];
```

The call to the function and resulting output follow.

Code 8.5.2:

```
x = [1:5];
[a b] = mean_and_trimmed_mean(x)
```

Output 8.5.2:

```
a =
      3
b =
      2.5000
```

8.6   Calling Functions Properly

It is worth taking a moment to emphasize the importance of calling functions properly. Not calling functions in the way they are designed to return outputs can lead to unexpected results.

Code 8.5.2 had the line `[a b] = mean_and_trimmed_mean(x)`. It was essential to declare the *pair* of output values to be returned by the function, because this particular function returned *two* values. If the call to `mean_and_trimmed_mean` did not list any output values or listed just one output value, only one value would be returned, namely, the first value returned by the function. The following code demonstrates what happens when different numbers of elements are indicated in calls to `mean_and_trimmed_mean`.

Code 8.6.1:

```
mean_and_trimmed_mean(x)
c = mean_and_trimmed_mean(x)
[d e] = mean_and_trimmed_mean(x)
[f g h] = mean_and_trimmed_mean(x)
```

Output 8.6.1:

```
ans =
      3

c =
      3

d =
      3

e =
      2.5000

??? Error using ==> mean_and_trimmed_mean
Too many output arguments.
```

8.7 Drawing on Previously Defined Functions Versus Creating Your Own

A final remark about functions is that there are two schools of thought about drawing on previously defined functions versus creating your own. Each approach has advantages and disadvantages.

MATLAB comes with a large number of functions, and people in the MATLAB programming community regularly provide functions for free over the world-wide web. It is certainly useful to draw on others' functions, particularly if creating those functions seems daunting or needlessly time-consuming.

On the other hand, using other people's functions can leave you at their mercy. You may be stuck with code that has a bug in it (though, admittedly, you may be capable of generating such code yourself, notwithstanding your use of this book ☺), and you might spend more time trying to find a function that does what you want than generating it yourself. I suggest that you create your own functions unless the functions you need are readily available from a trusted source.

8.8 Practicing Modules and Functions

Try your hand at the following exercises, using only the methods introduced so far in this book or given in the problems themselves.

Problem 8.8.1

Write a function to convert any specified value of a normally distributed random sample to a z score. The z score of such a value is its signed number of standard deviations away from the sample mean.

Problem 8.8.2

In Problems 5.8.2 and 5.8.3 you were asked to identify participants who had mean reaction times greater than 500 ms and proportions correct greater than .65. If you solved the problem and followed the instruction to use only material presented up to that point or to use only information given in the problems themselves, you did so without creating a function. Now write a function that takes as input: (a) the name of the matrix containing reaction times and proportions correct; (b) the reaction time cutoff; and (c) the proportion-correct cutoff. The function should return four matrices: (a) `Identified_Participants`; (b) `OK_Scores`; (c) `Mean_of_OK_reaction_times`; and (d) `Mean_Proportion_Correct`.

Problem 8.8.3

It would be desirable to apply the function you created in the last problem to a larger data set than the one given in Problem 5.8.2. You needn't collect actual data for this purpose. Instead, you can generate model data via simulation. Generate model data that reflect the following constraints: (a) There are 1000 trials; (b) The probability of a correct response on any given trial is .90; (c) Reaction times in correct trials are drawn from a normal distribution with mu = 700 ms and std = 20 ms; (d) Reaction times in incorrect trials are drawn from a normal distribution with mu = 600 ms and std = 80 ms; (e) Reaction times less than 0 ms are undefined. Generate the model data based on the above constraints with a single function that has arguments corresponding to the numbers mentioned in constraints 1 − 5.

Problem 8.6.4

Write a function to compute the probability of getting exactly k successes in n tries given the constraints outlined below. Quoting from an August 31, 2006 entry in Wikipedia (http://en.wikipedia.org/wiki/Binomial_distribution), "… if the random variable X follows the binomial distribution with parameters n and p, we write $X \sim B(n, p)$. The probability of getting exactly k successes is given by the probability mass function:

$$f(k; n, p) = \binom{n}{k} p^k (1-p)^{n-k}$$

for $k = 0, 1, 2, …, n$, where

$$\binom{n}{k} = \frac{n!}{k!(n-k)!} \; . \text{"}$$

Recall that $n!$ is called "n factorial" and is equal to $1 \times 2 \times 3 \times … \times (n-1) \times n$. Likewise, $k!$ is called "k factorial" and is equal to $1 \times 2 \times 3 \times … \times (k-1) \times k$.

Problem 8.6.5

In Problem 7.5.5 you were asked to write a program to administer a computerized questionnaire on a topic of interest to you. You were asked to use a structure data type and to allow participants to answer with whole sentences or phrases for at least some items. You were asked to save the data in an external file, and you were asked to record the times taken to answer the questions. Make this program modular and, having done so, take advantage of that modularity to pursue different lines of questions depending on participants' answers to particular questions.

9. Plots

The commands that are introduced and the sections in which they are premiered are as follows:

ylabel	(9.6)
legend	(9.7)
text	(9.8)
polyfit	(9.9)
box	(9.10)
grid	(9.10)
subplot	(9.10)
get(gca)	(9.12)
set	(9.12)
errorbar	(9.13)
polar	(9.14)
brighten	(9.15)
colormap	(9.15)
hist	(9.15)
bar	(9.16)
barh	(9.16)
feather	(9.17)
get(gcf)	(9.17)
pie	(9.17)
plotyy	(9.17)
print	(9.17)
quiver	(9.17)
set(gcf, position')	(9.17)
stairs	(9.17)
stem	(9.17)

9.1   Deciding to Plot Data and, for Starters, Generating a Sine Function

As mentioned in the Preface, one of MATLAB's most attractive features is that it lets you easily generate data plots and other graphics. This is the first chapter on this topic.

The first step in creating a data plot is deciding whether such a plot is worth creating. Looking at well-designed data plots either shows trends in your data or, when the data points look more like a blizzard than a line, that there is no trend.

Creating well-designed data plots takes practice, but MATLAB provides a convenient medium for honing your graphing skills

Let us create our first data plot. In Code 9.1.1, we first clear all variables, using `clear all`. Then we issue the `close all` command, which closes all currently active figures. Figures occur where plots and graphics appear. Using the `close all` command is advisable it you don't want to add a plot to an existing figure. The command `clf` lets us close just the currently active figure.

After saying `close all` in Code 9.1.1. we next indicate that we want to create figure number 1, using the command `figure(1)`. MATLAB assumes that the first figure number is 1, so we could just as well have written `figure`. However, it is useful to know about figure numbers in general in case you want to generate a series of figures such as `figure(2)`, `figure(3)`, and so on. Since you can activate individually numbered figure windows, you can also close individual figure windows. Thus, if you want to `close figure(3)`, you can say `close(figure(3))` or `close(3)` for short.

Via Code 9.1.1, we will generate the graph of a `sin` (pronounced "sine") function. To do so, we define a matrix `theta` as an array of 100 elements (all angles in this case) linearly spaced between $0 \times 2 \times$ `pi` and $4 \times 2 \times$ `pi`. The term `pi` (or π as is written in Greek notation and pronounced "pie" in English-speaking countries) refers to the ratio of the circumference of a circle to that circle's diameter. A diameter is 2 radiuses or 2 "radians" long, so the circumference of a circle has $2 \times$ `pi` radians.

For the graph we wish to generate, we want to go around a circle 4 times, taking 100 equal steps along the way. MATLAB assumes that angles increase in the counterclockwise direction and that an angle whose value is 0 is associated with the straight line extending from the center of the circle to the right. MATLAB uses radians (number of radiuses) rather than degrees in all of its trigonometric calculations. Pay close attention to that last statement, because forgetting it, and assuming that angles are being measured in degrees (180 degrees per radian or 360 degrees per 2 radians) can cause a lot of grief.

We wish to plot `sin(theta)` as a function of `theta` and we do so with the `plot` command. Keep in mind that the first argument provided to `plot` is the array for the horizontal axis or *abscissa* of the graph. The second argument provided to `plot` is the array for the vertical axis or *ordinate*.

Here, at long last, is the program. The last command, `shg`, tells MATLAB to bring up the active figure window, or `figure(1)` in this case. If `shg` were not included, the active window could remain behind other open windows.

Code 9.1.1

```
clear all
close all
figure(1)
theta = linspace(0,4*(2*pi),100);
plot(theta,sin(theta));
shg
```

Output 9.1.1

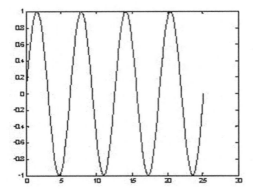

As seen in Output 9.1.1, the function `sin(theta)` oscillates around 0 with a maximum of 1 and a minimum of −1. This is because `sin(theta)` is obtained by taking the height (vertical position) of the end of the radius at a given angle `theta` and dividing that height by the (fixed) length of the radius. When `theta = 0/4 * 2*pi = 0*pi` radians (or 0 degrees), the height of the end of the radius is 0 times the radius; hence `sin(0*pi) = 0`. When `theta = 1/4 * 2*pi = .5*pi` radians (or 90 degrees), the height of the end of the radius is + 1 times the radius; hence `sin(.5*pi) = 1`. When `theta = 2/4 * 2*pi = 1*pi` radians (or 180 degrees), the height of the end of the radius is again 0 times the radius; hence `sin(1*pi) = 0`. When `theta = 3/4 * 2*pi = 1.5*pi` radians (or 270 degrees), the height of the end of the radius is −1 times the radius; hence `sin(1.5*pi ) = −1`. Finally, when `theta = 4/4 * 2*pi = 2*pi` radians (or 360 degrees), the height of the end of the radius is 0 times the radius; hence `sin(2*pi) = 0`. The `sin` function can keep on going forever, ascending and descending in a perfectly periodic fashion, which is why `sin` is called a periodic function.

9.2   Controlling Axes

Output 9.1.1 isn't as pretty as it might be. One problem is that the curve ends abruptly, leaving a great deal of room to spare. It would be nice to fix this and we can do so by controlling the axes, taking advantage of a function called `axis`. This function requires four elements: (a) the smallest value on the horizontal axis, (b) the largest value on the horizontal axis, (c) the smallest value on the vertical axis, and (d) the largest value on the vertical axis. In the code that follows, these four values are defined generically using the built-in functions `min` and `max` (see Chapter 3). Because the four elements constitute a matrix, they must be enclosed in brackets, as in any standard MATLAB matrix with more than a single element.

Code 9.2.1

```
figure(2)
y = sin(theta);
plot(theta,y);
axis([min(theta) max(theta) min(y) max(y)]);
shg
```

Output 9.2.1

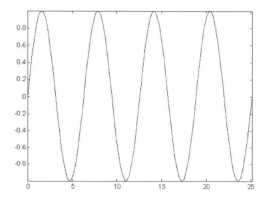

This graph looks better than its predecessor. However, it could be even prettier if we defined the axes so there were some "space to breathe" above and below the plotted points. In the next program we generalize the preceding code by adding more information concerning the minima and maxima for the x and y axes. We also illustrate another way of specifying these values that does not require the use of the **axis** command (not that there is anything wrong with the **axis** command). The alternative method is to use **xlim** and **ylim**. These functions have the advantage that they can be used independently of each other, allowing you to specify the limits of the x axis only or the y axis only. The **axis** command, by contrast, forces you to specify the limits of x *and* y.

Code 9.2.2

```
figure(3)
x = theta;
plot(x,y);
x_offset = 1;
y_offset = .2;
xlim([min(x) - x_offset, max(x+x_offset)]);
ylim([min(y) - y_offset, max(y+y_offset)]);
shg
```

Output 9.2.2

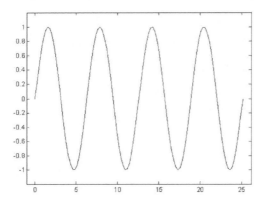

9.3   Controlling the Appearance of Plotted Points and Lines

You can control the way plotted points appear. Adding 'g—' to the `plot` command tells MATLAB to connect the points with a green (g) line (—). There is no need to specify `xlim` and `ylim` again, just as there is no need to specify `x` and `y` again because these values are active, owing to the fact that neither value has been cleared and we have not quit or restarted MATLAB. Quitting MATLAB clears all variables and figures.

In the program below, we introduce another new command, `hold on`, which tells MATLAB to maintain the already plotted figure when new material is added to it. In this case, blue o's are added to the graph. Note that these are blue letter-o's, not blue zeros. To see the o's in color rather than the grayscale used in this book, go to the book's website: www.matlab-behave.com

Code 9.3.1

```
figure(4);
plot(x,y,'g');
hold on;
plot(x,y,'bo');
shg;
```

Output 9.3.1

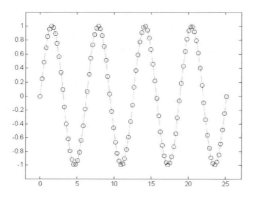

9.4   Having More Than One Graph Per Plot and More Types of Points and Lines

The `hold on` command is especially useful when you want to have more than one graph per plot. The program below shows how you can achieve this. We first tell MATLAB to create a new figure, `figure(5)`, and then issue a command to plot y against x using green o's and green line segments. Notice that the color and shape of the points as well as the line segments are indicated in a single command, `plot(x,y,'go-')`.

To illustrate what can be achieved with the `hold on` command, we add a second curve to `figure(5)`. Besides plotting `sin(x)` as a function of x, we also plot `cos(x)` as a function of x. `cos` is a built-in MATLAB function, just as is `sin`. `cos(x)`, pronounced "cosine of x," is obtained by taking the horizontal position of the end of the radius at a given angle theta and dividing the horizontal position by the fixed length of the radius.

As seen below, when we plot `cos(x)` as a function of x using blue line segments and blue squares (`'b-s'`), `cos(x)` is shifted horizontally relative to `sin(x)`.

Code 9.4.1

```
figure(5)
plot(x,y,'go-');
y = cos(x);
plot(x,y,'b-s');
shg
```

Output 9.4.1

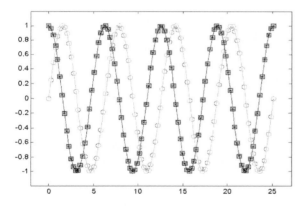

Why didn't we say `hold on` in the foregoing program? This was unnecessary because the `hold on` command was issued in the preceding program and remains on unless we change its state by typing `hold off` or, more simply, by typing `hold`, which toggles the state of `hold` from whatever it was before to its antithesis (from on to off or vice versa). It usually doesn't hurt to type `hold on` or `hold off` to make the code as clear as possible.

Code 9.4.2 shows that MATLAB plots can include a variety of colors and shapes of points and lines. So far we have used blue and green o's and squares, as well as blue and green line segments. By typing `help plot`, you can learn about the full range of plotting options that

MATLAB provides. Output 9.4.2 is an excerpt from the information that is returned when you type `help plot`.

Code 9.4.2

```
help plot
```

Output 9.4.2

```
Various line types, plot symbols and colors may be
obtained with PLOT(X,Y,S) where S is a character string
made from one element from any or all the following three
columns:

b    blue         .    point           -      solid
g    green        o    circle          :      dotted
r    red          x    x-mark          -.     dashdot
c    cyan         +    plus            --     dashed
m    magenta      *    star           (none)  no line
y    yellow       s    square
k    black        d    diamond
                  v    triangle (down)
                  ^    triangle (up)
                  <    triangle (left)
                  >    triangle (right)
                  p    pentagram
                  h    hexagram

For example, PLOT(X,Y,'c+:') plots a cyan dotted line
with a plus at each data point; PLOT(X,Y,'bd') plots blue
diamond at each data point but does not draw any line.
```

By drawing on the above information, you can specify other colors, shapes, and line types. The following program illustrates this point and also reveals another useful fact about plotting, namely that it is possible to tell MATLAB to generate two (or more) graphs with one `plot` command. Here, in one `plot` statement, we indicate that we wish to plot `sin(x)` against `x` using cyan plus signs connected by a dotted line, and that we also wish to plot `cos(x)` against `x` using red diamonds connected by no line. Both instructions can be given in one line of code.

Code 9.4.3

```
figure(6)
plot(x,sin(x),'c+:',x,cos(x),'rd');
shg
```

Output 9.4.3:

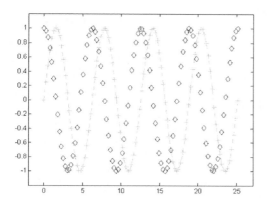

9.5   Getting and Setting Properties of Plotted Points

You can control the size of plotted points by using one of their properties: `markersize`. Setting `markersize` to 12 yields larger circles than the ones in the previous outputs.

Code 9.5.1

```
figure(7)
plot(x,sin(x),'ro-','markersize',12);
xlim([min(x) - x_offset, max(x+x_offset)]);
ylim([min(y) - y_offset, max(y+y_offset)]);
box on
shg
```

Output 9.5.1

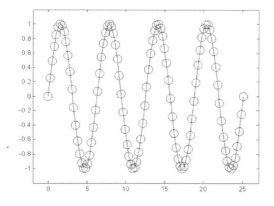

How do you find out about properties such as `markersize`? The answer is, with one of the most useful commands in MATLAB, `get`.

Code 9.5.2 shows how you can get the properties of a plot similar to the one above. The third line of Code 9.5.2 shows how the `get` command is used. `get` is a function whose argument (in this case h) is a set of parameters associated with the `plot` function, which is called in the second line of Code 9.5.2.

Output 9.5.2 includes text returned via `get(h)`. The graph reveals two things—first, that `sin(x)` plotted as a function of `cos(x)` yields a circle, and second, that the actual size of plotted points depends on the type of point as well as the value of `markersize`. Compare the size of the points in Output 9.5.2 with the size of the points in Output 9.5.1, where the value of `markersize` is the same but the types of plotted points are different.

Code 9.5.2

```
figure(8)
h = plot(cos(x),sin(x), 'r.','markersize',12);
get(h)
```

Output 9.5.2

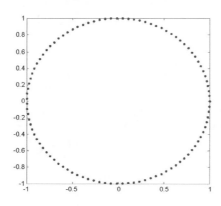

```
h =

                 Color:    [1 0 0]
             EraseMode:    'normal'
             LineStyle:    '-'
             LineWidth:    0.5000
                Marker:    'o'
            MarkerSize:    12
       MarkerEdgeColor:    'auto'
       MarkerFaceColor:    'none'
                 XData:    [1x100 double]
                 YData:    [1x100 double]
```

```
           ZData:   [1x0 double]
    BeingDeleted:   'off'
   ButtonDownFcn:   [ ]
        Children:   [0x1 double]
        Clipping:   'on'
       CreateFcn:   [ ]
       DeleteFcn:   [ ]
      BusyAction:   'queue'
HandleVisibility:   'on'
         HitTest:   'on'
   Interruptible:   'on'
        Selected:   'off'
SelectionHighlight:  'on'
             Tag:   ' '
            Type:   'line'
   UIContextMenu:   [ ]
        UserData:   [ ]
         Visible:   'on'
          Parent:   1.0710e+003
     DisplayName:   ' '
       XDataMode:   'manual'
     XDataSource:   ' '
     YDataSource:   ' '
     ZDataSource:   ' '
```

By knowing the properties of a `plot`, you can set the properties you want. For example, you can control the `markerfacecolor` of plotted points as well as the `markeredgecolor` of plotted points, as shown below. (The colors that appear are more vivid on the website than on this page.)

Code 9.5.3

```
figure(9)
plot(x,y,'g—');
hold on
x_offset = 0;
y_offset = .2;
axis([min(x)—x_offset, max(x)+x_offset, …
     min(y)—y_offset, max(y+y_offset)]);
plot(x,y,'o', 'color','r','markersize',6, …
     'markeredgecolor','k','markerfacecolor','r');
```

Output 9.5.3

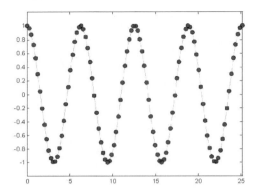

Changing the `markerfacecolor` and the `markeredgecolor` of plotted points is just one thing that can be done by varying figure properties. The method illustrated in Code 9.5.3 can be generalized to other properties of interest. For example, `color` can be specified as shown in Code 9.5.3, where `'color'` is followed by a single letter code such as `'r'`. Alternatively `'color'` can be followed by a 3 × 1 matrix such as `[1 0 0]`. The first number is the value of red, the second number is the value of green, and the third number is the value is blue. It is easy to remember this order by memorizing the letters RGB. A further mnemonic aid is to think of RGB as the initials of the fictional character Roy G. Biv. Setting each of the three numbers associated with `'color'` to values between 0 and 1 lets you create almost any color you wish. Only values between 0 and 1 are permissible as values for `'color'`. Each is a proportion.

9.6   **Adding** `xlabels`, `ylabels`, **and** `titles`

You can generate a graph like the one shown in Output 9.5.3 by adding an `xlabel`, a `ylabel`, and a `title`.

Code 9.6.1

```
figure(10)
plot(x,y,'g-');
hold on
x_offset = 0;
y_offset = .2;
axis([min(x) − x_offset, max(x)+x_offset, …
     min(y)−y_offset, max(y+y_offset)]);
plot(x,y,'o','color','r','markersize',6, …
     'markeredgecolor','k','markerfacecolor','r');
xlabel('Time');
ylabel('Happiness');
title('Life has its ups and downs');
```

Output 9.6.1

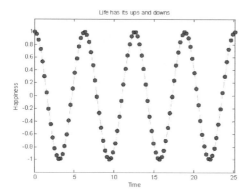

9.7   Adding Legends

You can also add a `legend` to a graph, as in the following example, where hypothetical learning curves are generated for participants in four conditions, `c1`, `c2`, `c3`, and `c4`. The participants try to recall the same items after the items are presented in identical fashion in successive trials. The learning curves are based on the idea that the four conditions have different asymptotes (maximum items recalled in this case) and that the rate at which the asymptotes are approached diminishes the longer the experiment continues.

In creating a legend, we assign strings to each curve. The order of the strings should correspond to the order in which the data are plotted. This is why the order of plotting the curves below is "backwards." We plot the curves in an order that ensures good stimulus-response compatibility between the items in the legend and the curves themselves (the higher the legend, the higher the curve). The arguments at the end of the `legend` command tell MATLAB where to place the legend. Other options for legend placements are available. For more information about legends, type `help legend` at the MATLAB command line.

Code 9.7.1

```
figure(11)
max_learn = [10 11 12 13];
trial = [1:10];
c1 = max_learn(1) - exp(-trial);
c2 = max_learn(2) - exp(-trial);
c3 = max_learn(3) - exp(- trial);
c4 = max_learn(4) - exp(- trial);

hold on
plot(trial,c4,'g-^');
plot(trial,c3,'m—');
plot(trial,c2,'b-.>');
plot(trial,c1,'k:v');
legend('Group 4','Group 3',…
    'Group 2','Group 1', …
    'Location','EastOutside');
```

Output 9.7.1

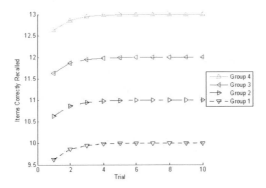

9.8   Adding Text

You can add text to a figure. In the following example, we plot a power function and an exponential function. A power function is one in which the independent variable is raised to some numerical power. The time it takes to perform a task usually diminishes with practice in a way that follows a power function. An exponential function is one in which the independent variable is itself part of the exponent to which some quantity is raised, as in the learning example above.

In the code that follows, we label the two curves using the `text` command, which has three arguments: (a) the horizontal position where the text begins; (b) the vertical position where the text begins; and (c) the actual text string. In Code 9.8.1, we add a vertical offset and a horizontal offset to avoid crowding the text onto the curves. The vertical offset and horizontal offset were found through trial and error.

Code 9.8.1

```
figure(12)

a = 1;              % starting value
b = .5;             % rate parameter
xx = [0:20];
vert_offset = .05;
hor_offset = .50;

y_power = a * xx.^-b;
y_exp = a * exp(b*-xx);

hold on
box on
plot(y_power,'mo-');
plot(y_exp,'kd-');
```

```
hor_p = xx(5) + hor_offset;
vert_p = y_power(5) + vert_offset;
text(hor_p,vert_p,'Power function');

hor_e = xx(6) + hor_offset;
vert_e = y_exp(6) + vert_offset;
text(hor_e,vert_e,'Exponential function');
```

Output 9.8.1

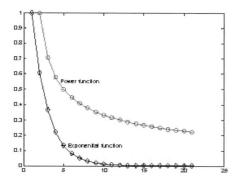

9.9   Fitting Curves

Behavioral scientists often fit curves to observed points. One way to do this is to use the `polyfit` function. This function lets you fit a polynomial function to data. A polynomial function of a variable `x` is a sum of terms consisting of a coefficient, often called `a0`, times `x` raised to the 0 power, plus another coefficient, often called `a1`, times `x` raised to the 1 power, plus another coefficient, often called `a2`, times `x` raised to the 2 power, all the way up to a coefficient, often called `an`, times `x` raised to the n power:

```
y = (a0 * x^0) + (a1 * x^1) + (a2 * x^2) + … + (an * x^n)
```

Because any value raised to the 0 power is 1, `x^0 = 1`, in which case `(a0 * x^0) = a0`. Note that n defines the "order" of the polynomial.

In the following example we create a set of dummy data based on a new matrix `x`, which runs from –20 to +20. To create the dummy data, we put each value of `x` through a second-order polynomial function to yield `y`, and then we add normally distributed random numbers to `y`, scaled by a coefficient arbitrarily called `randn_coeff`.

The first time we fit a curve to these data, we find a matrix of coefficients, called `fitted_coefficients` which allows for a best fit of a first-order polynomial function. This is done with `polyfit(x,y,1)`. The last term, 1, defines the order of the polynomial. A polynomial of order 1, or a "first-order polynomial," is also called a linear equation. The best-fitting coefficients in this example are used to generate a matrix of theoretical values called `y_hat1`.

Code 9.9.1

```
clear x y
a3 = 0;
a2 = 1;
a1 = 1;
a0 = 0;
x = [− 20:20];
randn_coeff = 60;

y = a3*x.^3 + a2*x.^2 + a1*x.^1 + a0*x.^0;
r = rand(length(y))*randn_coeff;
r = r(1,:);
y = y + r;

fitted_coefficients = polyfit(x,y,1);
y_hat1 = fitted_coefficients(1)*x.^1 + …
         fitted_coefficients(2)*x.^0;

figure (13)

hold on
plot(y,'bo');         % show original data
plot(y_hat1,'r-');    % show fitted points joined by a line
xlim([0 length(x)]);
box on                % put a box around the graph
c = corrcoef(y, y_hat1);
message = ['Straight line fit: r^2 = …
    ',num2str(c(1,2)^2,3)];
title(message);
```

Output 9.9.1

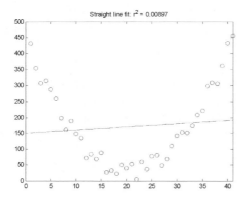

As seen above, the fit isn't very good. The proportion of variance accounted for by the linear function, r^2, is only .00897. To find r^2 (also known as the *coefficient of determination*), we computed the correlation matrix, arbitrarily called c, between y and y_hat1 using corrcoef. We squared the element in the first row and second column of c to obtain r^2 (or we could have equally well squared the element in the second row and first column of c). To convert the value of r^2 to a string, suitable for presentation with the title command, we used the num2str command. The final term in the num2str command was used to define the number of significant figures.

Next we seek a better fit with a second-order polynomial, also called a quadratic equation. We find a matrix of coefficients, arbitrarily called pp2, that allows for a best fit of a second-order polynomial function. This is done using the command polyfit(x,y,2). The coefficients are used to generate a matrix of theoretical values called y_hat2.

Code 9.9.2

```
clear fitted_coefficients;
fitted_coefficients = polyfit(x,y,2);
y_hat2 = fitted_coefficients(1)*x.^2 + …
        fitted_coefficients(2)*x.^1 + …
        fitted_coefficients(3)*x.^0;

figure (14)
hold on
plot(y,'bo');          % show original data
plot(y_hat2,'r-');     % show fitted points joined by a line
xlim([0 length(x)]);
box on                 % put a box around the graph
c = corrcoef(y, y_hat2);
message = ['Quadratic fit: r^2 = ',num2str(c(1,2)^2,3)];
title(message);
```

Output 9.9.2

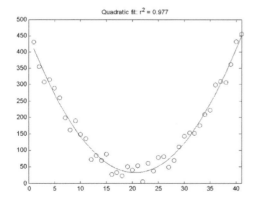

The quadratic equation provides a much better fit to the data. The proportion of variance accounted for by the quadratic function is nearly .98.

9.10   Creating Subplots and Turning Grids, Boxes, and Axes On and Off

You can generate several subplots within a figure using MATLAB's subplot function. This function has three arguments. The first is the number of subplot rows. The second is the number of subplot columns. The third is the number of the subplot that is about to be plotted, where this number increases from left to right and from top to bottom.

In the example that follows, we generate a 4 × 1 matrix of subplots. The first subplot, designated by `subplot(4,1,1)` has the characteristic that a grid is on. The second subplot, designated by `subplot(4,1,2)` has the characteristic that a box surrounds the graph. The third subplot, designated by `subplot(4,1,3)` has the characteristic that there is no axis. The fourth subplot, designated by `subplot(4,1,4)` forces the graph to be square. Note that `subplot` does not actually plot data. The plot command does that and is issued after the `subplot` command informs MATLAB which particular subplot is to be plotted next.

Code 9.10.1

```
figure(15)

subplot(4,1,1)
plot(cos(x),'r.','markersize',12);
grid on

subplot(4,1,2)
plot(cos(x),'r.','markersize',12);
box on

subplot(4,1,3)
plot(cos(x),'r.','markersize',12);
axis off

subplot(4,1,4)
plot(cos(x),'r.','markersize',12);
axis square
```

Output 9.10.1

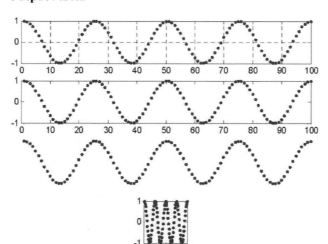

9.11 Exploiting Matrix Assignments to Merge Subplots

Because subplots appear in positions occupying matrices, you can merge subplots to enjoy considerable flexibility in the way the subplots appear. You can do this by using the methods covered in Chapter 3 for addressing different elements of a matrix.

In the example that follows, we create a figure with a large title across the top (occupying subplots 1 and 2 of the 4×2 matrix of subplots to be drawn), and, among the other subplots to be drawn, we generate a graph in matrix positions 5 and 7. The function used to place letters in the panels appears in Code 9.11.2.

Before showing the code used to generate the subplots (Code 9.11.1), it is worth mentioning that some of the features of the code were based on trial and error. For instance, the number of spaces before the word `Banner` was adjusted by trying out different numbers of spaces, and the value of .90 in the call to `text_in_box` for panel C was changed from the value of .80 used in all the other panels because the appearance of .80 didn't turn out as nicely as I wanted. Trial and error adjustment of parameters is often the most expedient, if not the most elegant, method of parameter specification.

Code 9.11.1

```
figure(16)
clear x y
x = [1:10];
y = x + 1;
subplot(4,2,1:2); %  In the 4 rows and 2 columns of subplots,
                  %  subplots 1 and 2
xlim([0 1]);
ylim([0 1]);
axis off
text(−.05,.05,        'A Banner Year','fontsize',24);

subplot(4,2,3);   %  In the 4 rows and 2 columns of subplots,
                  %  subplot 3
plot(x,y,'k')
text_in_box(.05,.80,'A')

subplot(4,2,4);   %  In the 4 rows and 2 columns of subplots,
                  %  subplot 4
plot(x,y,'k')
text_in_box(.05,.80,'B')

subplot(4,2,[5 7]);%  In the 4 rows and 2 columns of subplots,
                  %  subplots 5 and 7
plot(x,y,'k')
text_in_box(.05,.90,'C')

subplot(4,2,6);   %  In the 4 rows and 2 columns of subplots,
                  %  subplot 6
plot(x,y,'k')
text_in_box(.05,.80,'D')
subplot(4,2,8);   %  In the 4 rows and 2 columns of subplots,
                  %  subplot 8
```

```
plot(x,y,'k')
text_in_box(.05,.80,'E')
```

Code 9.11.2

```
function text_in_box(x_place,y_place,s)

xs = xlim;
ys = ylim;
text(x_place*xs(2),y_place*ys(2),s);
```

Output 9.11.2

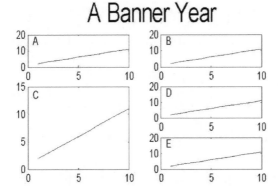

9.12   Getting and Setting Properties of Axes

Just as you can get the properties of plotted points by using the get function, you can get the properties of the axes of graphs with the get(gca) command. gca denotes the properties or "handles" of the current axes. Here get(gca) is issued after running Code 9.10.1.

Code 9.12.1

```
get(gca)
```

Output 9.12.1

```
ActivePositionProperty = outerposition
ALim = [0 1]
ALimMode = auto
AmbientLightColor = [1 1 1]
Box = on
CameraPosition = [12.5664 0.000251729 17.3205]
CameraPositionMode = auto
CameraTarget = [12.5664 0.000251729 0]
```

```
CameraTargetMode = auto
CameraUpVector = [0 1 0]
CameraUpVectorMode = auto
CameraViewAngle = [6.60861]
CameraViewAngleMode = auto
CLim = [0 1]
CLimMode = auto
Color = [1 1 1]
CurrentPoint = [ (2 by 3) double array]
ColorOrder = [ (7 by 3) double array]
DataAspectRatio = [12.5664 1.19975 1]
DataAspectRatioMode = auto
DrawMode = normal
FontAngle = normal
FontName = Helvetica
FontSize = [10]
FontUnits = points
FontWeight = normal
GridLineStyle = :
Layer = bottom
LineStyleOrder = —
LineWidth = [0.5]
MinorGridLineStyle = :
NextPlot = add
OuterPosition = [0 0 1 1]
PlotBoxAspectRatio = [1 1 1]
PlotBoxAspectRatioMode = auto
Projection = orthographic
Position = [0.13 0.11 0.775 0.815]
TickLength = [0.01 0.025]
TickDir = in
TickDirMode = auto
TightInset = [0.0928571 0.0904762 0.00357143 0.0547619]
Title = [1387]
Units = normalized
View = [0 90]
XColor = [0 0 0]
XDir = normal
XGrid = off
XLabel = [1385]
XAxisLocation = bottom
XLim = [0 25.1327]
XLimMode = manual
XMinorGrid = off
XMinorTick = off
XScale = linear
XTick = [ (1 by 12) double array]
XTickLabel = [ (12 by 2) char array]
XTickLabelMode = auto
```

```
XTickMode = manual
YColor = [0 0 0]
YDir = normal
YGrid = off
YLabel = [1386]
YAxisLocation = left
YLim = [- 1.1995 1.2]
YLimMode = manual
YMinorGrid = off
YMinorTick = off
YScale = linear
YTick = [ (1 by 11) double array]
YTickLabel = [ (11 by 4) char array]
YTickLabelMode = auto
YTickMode = auto
ZColor = [0 0 0]
ZDir = normal
ZGrid = off
ZLabel = [1388]
ZLim = [- 1 1]
ZLimMode = auto
ZMinorGrid = off
ZMinorTick = off
ZScale = linear
ZTick = [- 1 0 1]
ZTickLabel =
ZTickLabelMode = auto
ZTickMode = auto

BeingDeleted = off
ButtonDownFcn =
Children = [ (2 by 1) double array]
Clipping = on
CreateFcn =
DeleteFcn =
BusyAction = queue
HandleVisibility = on
HitTest = on
Interruptible = on
Parent = [9]
Selected = off
SelectionHighlight = on
Tag =
Type = axes
UIContextMenu = [ ]
UserData = [ ]
Visible = on
```

Seeing this long list shows what a wealth of options are associated with plot. Looking through the list, you see some terms you have already encountered, such as xlim and ylim, but many news ones are there as well.

To illustrate how you can make use of the properties in this list, the next program shows how you can control the tick marks in a graph. You can do this using the set function. set is an important function because it can be used flexibly in connection with any object property of interest, such as the axes of the current figure. Code 9.12.2 exploits this capability by indicating that the xticks run from 2 to 24 in increments of 2.

Code 9.12.2

```
figure(17)
x = linspace(0,4*(2*pi),100);
y = sin(x);
plot(x,y);
plot(x,y,'g-');
hold on
x_offset = 0;
y_offset = .2;
axis([min(x)- x_offset, max(x)+x_offset, …
      min(y)- y_offset, max(y+y_offset)]);
plot(x,y,'o','color','r','markersize',6, …
      markeredgecolor','k','markerfacecolor','r');
xlabel('Time');
ylabel('Happiness');
title('Life has its ups and downs.');
set(gca,'xtick',[2:2:24]);

shg
```

Output 9.12.2

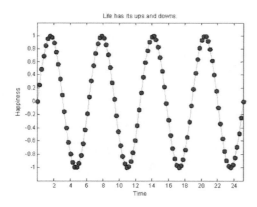

Here is another example, in which tick marks are suppressed entirely, as can be useful when you want to show a qualitative relation. (I often show such graphs in my undergraduate teaching). Only the last line, concerning xtick, has been changed from Code 9.12.3, and a new line, concerning ytick, has been added.

Code 9.12.3

```
figure(18)
plot(x,y,'g-');
hold on
x_offset = 0;
y_offset = .2;
axis([min(x)- x_offset, max(x)+x_offset, …
     min(y)- y_offset, max(y+y_offset)]);
plot(x,y,'o','color','r','markersize',6, …
     'markeredgecolor','k','markerfacecolor','r');
xlabel('Time');
ylabel('Happiness');
title('Life has its ups and downs.');
set(gca,'xtick',[ ]);
set(gca,'ytick',[ ]);
```

Output 9.12.3

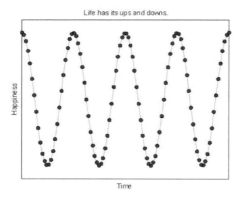

9.13   Plotting Data Points With Error Bars

It is often desirable to show how variable data are by including error bars – for example, bars that extend above and below a depicted mean by an amount equal to the standard deviation of the associated sample.

Code 9.13.1 shows how you can display error bars using MATLAB's errorbar command. This command takes three arguments—the horizontal position of each point (x), the vertical position of each point (y), and the length of the bar itself (sd). As shown in Code 9.13.1, the color of the bars can be indicated as well. Here we request black ('k') bars.

When the `errorbar` function is used, it tends to connect successive data points with lines. To hide these lines, you can then tell MATLAB to connect successive data points with white lines (`'w—'`), as in the code below.

Code 9.13.1

```
figure(19)
x= [1:10];
y = [4 11 25 65 141 191 313 301 487 673];
sd = [52 53 49 59 60 58 55 57 53 61];
box on
hold on
errorbar(x,y,sd,'k','markersize',18)
plot(x,y','w-',x,y,'k.','markersize',18)
shg
```

Output 9.13.1

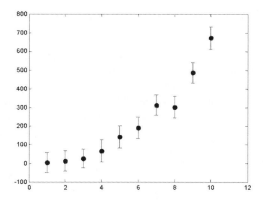

9.14   Generating Polar Plots

So far we have only plotted data in Cartesian coordinates (i.e., rectilinear frames of reference). For data that can be characterized in terms of an *angle* and a magnitude, it is possible to plot the data in *polar* coordinates. In these so-called polar plots, each point is positioned some distance (or magnitude) away from the origin along a line with a specified angle relative to the line extending from the origin to the right.

Code 9.14.1:

```
figure(20)
clear h i
h= [0:.1:2]*pi;
polar(h,h,'ko');
shg
```

Output 9.14.1:

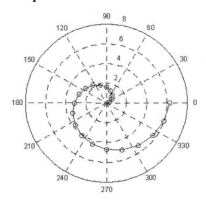

9.15   Generating Histograms

Another kind of graph supported by MATLAB is the histogram. A histogram shows the number of elements in bins of data.

Code 9.15.1 shows how to generate a histogram using the `hist` command. We generate a 1 x 2000 matrix of normally distributed random numbers using `randn`. Then we use the `hist` function to return two outputs. One is N, a matrix whose elements are the number of values in each of the 10 bins that `hist` creates by default. The other is X, a matrix whose elements are the means of the values in each of the 10 bins. When `hist` is called again with no explicit outputs, it yields a graph. The colors of the bars in the graph can be set to grey via the command `colormap([.5 .5 .5])`. These numbers signify that in this particular case the values of red, green, and blue are all .5. The bars can be brightened by, say, 75% using the command `brighten(.75)`.

Code 9.15.1:

```
figure(21)
randn('state',sum(100*clock))
h = randn(1,2000);
[N,X] = hist(h,6)
hist(h)
colormap([.5 .5 .5])
brighten(.75)
```

Output 9.15.1:

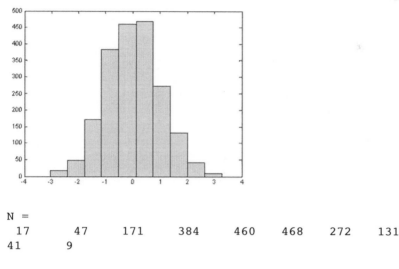

```
N =
   17        47       171       384       460       468       272       131
   41         9

X =
  −2.7307  −2.0986  −1.4665  −0.8344  −0.2023  0.4298  1.0619  1.6940
   2.3261   2.9582
```

9.16   Generating Bar Graphs

Histograms are just one kind of bar graph. Code 9.16.1 yields another kind. Here we generate horizontal bars using the `barh` function. (Vertical bars are generated with `bar`.) The
bars are grey, as in the last example, but I have also included, in the form of comments, the
values of `colormap` that yield black, bars, white bars, red bars, green bars, and blue bars.
The value assigned to `brighten` is smaller than before and the bars are, accordingly,
darker than in Output 9.15.1.

Code 9.16.1:

```
figure(22)
a = [[3 4 5 6 7 6 5 4 3]];
barh(a)
colormap([.5 .5 .5])      %  gray bars
%   colormap([0 0 0])     %  black bars
%   colormap([1 1 1])     %  white bars
%   colormap([1 0 0])     %  red bars
%   colormap([0 1 0])     %  green bars
%   colormap([0 0 1])     %  blue bars
brighten(.15)
ylim([0 ,10])
xlim([0 8])
```

Output 9.16.1:

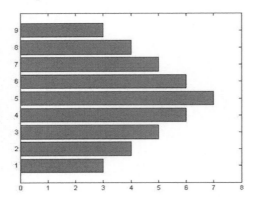

9.17   Exporting and Printing Figures

How do you export and print figures from MATLAB?

The simplest method (the one I used to put figures into this book) is to manually copy one figure at a time and paste it into the document you are producing (e.g., the Word document for the grant proposal you are writing). To do this, with the figure window open, click on the Edit icon of the toolbar and then click on Copy Figure. Prior to doing this, you can click on Copy Options to set your preferences for how the figure should be copied. You can also save the current figure using `save as`.

Another, more automatic, method is to use the `print` command, as in the following examples. In the first one, `figure(23)` is printed (`23`) at 600 pixel resolution (`'– r600'`) to a `jpeg` file (`'–djpeg'`) named `my_first_figure_print_23`. In the second example, `figure(24)` is printed (`24`) at 800 pixel resolution (`'– r800'`) to a `tif` file (`'–dtiff'`) named `my_second_figure_print_24`. By default, the files are printed to the current directory. You can check that the files are printed with the `ls` command, though the check is only complete when the files have been opened and individually inspected.

Code 9.17.1:

```
figure(23)
plot([1:10],[1:10].^– 3,'k-o')
print (23, '– r600', '– djpeg', 'my_first_figure_print_23')

figure(24)
plot([1:10],[1:10].^– 2,'k-s')
print (24, '–r800', '– dtiff', 'my_second_figure_print_24')

ls *.jpg
ls *.tif
```

Output 9.17.1:

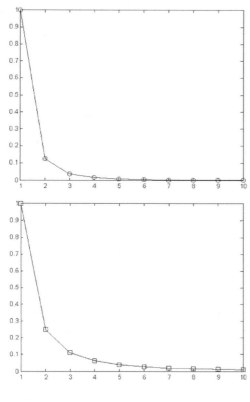

```
my_first_figure_print.jpg
my_second_figure_print.tif
```

9.18   Generating Other Kinds of Graphs and Getting and Setting Figure Properties

Several final remarks are worth making. First, most of the techniques described earlier for regular line graphs also apply to bars and histograms. For example, you can use `xlabel`, `ylabel`, and `title` with bars and histograms. The best way to see what works is to experiment.

Second, there are other plot options that you can explore for yourself. If you want to have different coordinates on the left and right vertical axes, you can use `plotyy`. MATLAB also lets you make special plots based on the `stairs` command, the `stem` command, the `pie` command, the `feather` command, and the `quiver` command. You should know enough about plotting from this chapter to explore these other options on your own.

Third, `get(gcf)` gets you properties (or "handles") of the current figure. After you have used `get(gcf)`, you can `set` properties of interest to control those properties. For example, you can control the size the figure on the computer screen with a command like this.

Code 9.18.1:

```
set(gcf, 'position', [464 581 672 504])
```

The values in the array are, respectively, the horizontal and vertical positions of the lower left corner and the horizontal and vertical positions of the upper right corner. You can find values you like by manually repositioning a figure as you like it, then use `get(gcf, 'position')` to determine what those pleasing values are. Finally, you can enter those values into code such as Code 9.17.1.

Fourth and finally, this chapter has only scratched the surface of the things that can be done with plots in MATLAB. Because the aim of this book is to equip you with the intellectual tools needed to get you started with MATLAB, you will hopefully know enough from this chapter to create your own two-dimensional graphs and make sense of the wealth of information in MATLAB's Help documents that indicate what else can be done to plot data.

9.19 Practicing Plots

Try your hand at the following exercises, using only the methods introduced so far in this book or in information given in the problems themselves.

Problem 9.19.1

The following code yields one bell-shaped curve. Modify the code to get two bell-shaped curves, with one shifted .5 units to the right of the other, as shown in the figure after the code below. Have the plot appear in `figure(1)`.

```
figure(1)
x = linspace(0,1,200);
a = 6;
b = 6;
y = (x.^a).*((1-x).^b);
plot(x,y,'k')
```

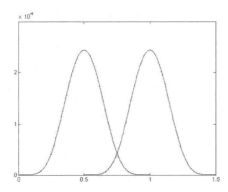

Problem 9.19.2

Problem 5.8.5 referred to the equation

```
p_correct = base_rate + learning_rate*log(trial),
```

where `trial` could take on the values 1, 2, 3, ..., 200, `learning_rate` could be any real number between 0 and 1, `base_rate` was ¼, and `p_correct` could not exceed 1. Generate a figure resembling the one below by setting `learning_rate` to .02. Plot `p_correct` as a function of `trial`, label the x axis `Trials`, label the y axis `Proportion Correct`, and have the title say `Learning`. Have the points appear as black o's connected with line segments. The `grid` should be on, the `box` should be on, the plot should appear in `figure(2)`, and the plot should look like this

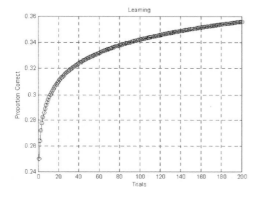

Problem 9.19.3

Adapt the program you wrote for the last problem to generate a figure resembling the one below by setting `learning_rate` to .02, .04, and .06. Have the plot appear in `figure(3)`.

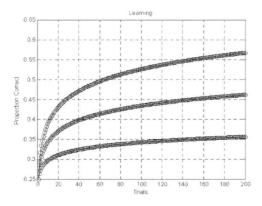

Problem 9.19.4

Adapt the program you wrote for the last problem to generate a figure resembling the one below by again setting `learning_rate` to .02, .04, and .06 and making the subplots on the right show the cumulative proportions correct for each of the three learning rates. Have the plot appear in `figure(4)`.

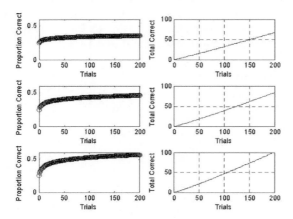

Problem 9.19.5

Adapt the program you wrote for the last problem to generate a figure that resembles the one below. There are two new features of the figure to be generated. One is that the learning rates are specified as text in each of the left subplots. The other is that the subplots on the right include a star at the trial for which the cumulative proportion correct exceeds 50. Have the plot appear in `figure(5)`.

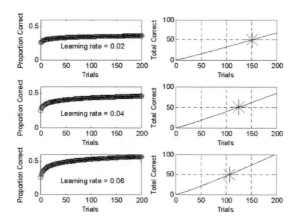

10. Lines, Shapes, and Images

The commands that are introduced and the sections in which they are premiered are as follows:

`set(gca)`	(10.1)
`set(gcf)`	(10.1)
`axis square`	(10.2)
`fill`	(10.2)
`image`	(10.3)
`imread`	(10.3)
`fontsize`	(10.4)
`ginput`	(10.4)
`rotation`	(10.4)
`saveas`	(10.5)

10.1   Generating Lines

Chapter 9 was concerned with data plots, which can include lines, shapes, or images. The latter elements can also stand alone for experiments or other purposes. This chapter is concerned with the manipulation of lines, shapes, and images in MATLAB.

Let us begin with lines. We generated lines with the `plot` command in Chapter 9 (e.g., Output 9.8.1). In the rest of this section, we focus further on line generation using the `plot` command.

In Code 10.1.1, we `clear` all variables, `close` all figure windows, and then provide instructions for drawing a line in `figure(1)`. We use the `plot` command, recalling that this command takes two arguments: an x (abscissa) array and a y (ordinate) array. Here we limit the x array to just two values, the starting and ending values of x, and we likewise limit the y array to two values, the starting and ending values of y. We assign `plot(x,y)` to a variable called `our_first_line`. For aesthetic reasons only, we indicate that we want the graph to be enclosed in a box.

Code 10.1.1

```
clear all
close all
figure(1)
x = [0 1];
y = [0 1];
our_first_line = plot(x, y);
box on
```

Output 10.1.1

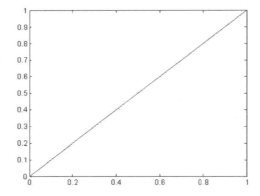

We can discover the properties of our_first_line by calling the get function.

Code 10.1.2

```
get(our_first_line)
```

Output 10.1.2

```
Color = [0 0 1]
EraseMode = normal
LineStyle = —
LineWidth = [0.5]
Marker = none
MarkerSize = [6]
MarkerEdgeColor = auto
MarkerFaceColor = none
XData = [0 1]
YData = [0 1]
ZData = [ ]

BeingDeleted = off
ButtonDownFcn =
MChildren = [ ]
```

```
Clipping = on
CreateFcn =
DeleteFcn =
BusyAction = queue
HandleVisibility = on
HitTest = on
Interruptible = on
Parent = [151.008]
Selected = off
SelectionHighlight = on
Tag =
Type = line
UIContextMenu = [ ]
UserData = [ ]
Visible = on
```

Having discovered that a property of `our_first_line` is `color`, we can specify the `color` for a new plot, to be assigned to the variable `our_second_line`. The new plot is displayed in `figure(2)`. Note that we have to issue the `box on` command again if we want the box to be on, because `box` is set to off each time a new figure window is opened. By saying `'color', [1  0  0]`, we indicate that we want the value of red to be 1 and the values of green and blue to be 0. In the last example, the line was blue, as indicated by the first line of Output 10.1.2, `Color = [0 0 1]`. The line appeared in this book as black, but the actual, intended color can be seen on the book's website (www.matlab-behave.com)

Code 10.1.3

```
figure(2)
delta_y = .5;
our_second_line = plot([min(x) max(x)], Y
    [min(y)+ delta_y max(y) + delta_y],'color',[1 0 0]);
box on
```

Output 10.1.3

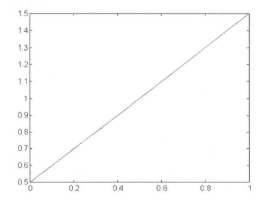

Having discovered that another property of our_first_line is linestyle, we can specify a new linestyle and, for that matter, a new color and linewidth. In Code 10.1.4, we specify these values for our_third_line, to be drawn in figure(3). We use the set command rather than the get command this time, partly to be reminded that this is another way of specifying figure properties. We also experiment with new values of color so that the red, green, and blue elements of the color matrix are not just assigned 1's and 0's. The following color values make for a bright brown which can be seen more easily on the website (www.matlab-behave.com) than on this printed page.

Code 10.1.4

```
figure(3)
delta_y = 1;
our_third_line = plot([min(x) max(x)], …
    [min(y)+ 2*delta_y max(y) + 2*delta_y]);
set(our_third_line,'color',[.9 .5 .1], …
    'linestyle','—', …
    'linewidth',8);
box on
```

Output 10.1.4

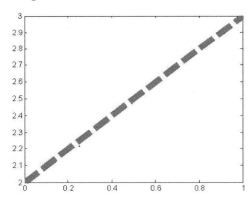

A further use of set not mentioned previously is that when set is used instead of get, MATLAB lists all the possible properties of the argument of set. If you type

Code 10.1.5

```
set(our_third_line)
```

the output is long. I have suppressed it here.

If you don't want all the properties of a plot but you want specific properties, you can type set(gcf) to find out about figure properties, or set(gca) to find out about axis properties. You can find out about specific figure properties or specific axis properties by adding optional strings that refer to them, as in the two examples below.

Code 10.1.6

```
set(gca,'XGrid')
set(gcf,'PaperOrientation')
```

Output 10.1.6

```
[ on | {off} ]
[ {portrait} | landscape | rotated ]
```

Output 10.1.6 gives the possible values of the properties in question. The values in brackets are the default values (the values MATLAB provides when no specific, alternative instructions are given).

10.2   Forming and Filling Shapes

Shapes are enclosed n-sided polygons, where n >= 3 is the number of straight line segments enclosing the polygon. Thus, a triangle is an n = 3 shape, a rectangle is an n = 4 shape, and so on. When the lengths of the straight line segments are equal, the n = 3 shape is an equilateral triangle, the n = 4 shape is a square, and so on.

MATLAB provides a function called `fill` which lets you form and color shapes. We use the `fill` function in Code 10.2.1 within a function called `my_polygon_1`, which takes three arguments. The first is the number of sides, n, of the polygon to be filled. The second is the distance, r, of each vertex of the polygon from the polygon's center (e.g., the radius of a circle when n is so large that the generated shape is visually indistinguishable from a circle). The third argument is the 3 × 1 RGB color matrix defining the color (i.e., the first number defines the proportion of red, the second number defines the proportion of green, and the third number defines the proportion of blue). `my_polygon_ 1` uses an x matrix and a y matrix as well as some trigonometry (see sections 9.1 and 9.4) for generality. We add 1 to n because n + 1 vertices are needed to generate n sides. The call to `my_poly-gon_1` is shown in Code 10.2.2, where we indicate that in `figure(4)`, we wish to fill a four-sided polygon whose "radius" has length 1, and whose color is given by the matrix `[.5 .5 .5]`. We also use `axis square` to keep the current axes the same size. For other axis options, use `help axis`.

Code 10.2.1

```
function my_polygon_1(n,r,c)

x = linspace(0,2*pi,n+1)
x = r*cos(x

y = linspace(0,2*pi,n+1)
y = r*sin(y);

fill(x,y,c)
```

Code 10.2.2

```
figure(4)
my_polygon_1(4,1,[.5 .5 .5])
axis square
```

Output 10.2.2

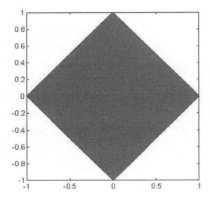

The four-sided polygon in Output 10.2.2 is a diamond. If you want a square, you need to rotate the shape. In my_polygon_2 we add a fourth argument that provides for such rotation. The fourth argument, called turn, shifts the series of angles used to define x and y. The new computation that uses turn is designed so you can set the fourth term to 0 for the default orientation. Calls to my_polygon_2 are shown in Code 10.2.4, where the angles increase from a negative value up to 0 so a square is the last polygon drawn, making it the one that sits "on top" of the others.

Code 10.2.3

```
function my_polygon_2(n,r,c,turn)

x = linspace(0,2*pi,n+1)
x = x + (turn + 1/(2*n))*(2*pi);
x = r*cos(x);

y = linspace(0,2*pi,n+1)
y = y + (turn + 1/(2*n))*(2*pi);
y = r*sin(y);

fill(x,y,c)
```

Code 10.2.4

```
figure(5)
hold on
for turn = linspace(−.2,0,5)
    my_polygon_2(4,1,[.5 .5 .5],turn)
    axis off
    end
```

Output 10.2.4

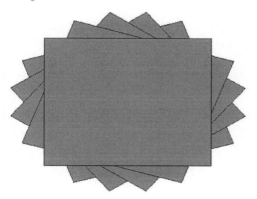

The `fill` command applies to irregular polygons and even to closed forms whose line segments cross, as illustrated in Code 10.2.5, where "crazy" series of **x** and **y** values are used. In addition, a property of the object being drawn—the width of the edge line—is specified through the `set` command.

Code 10.2.5

```
figure(6)
crazy_x = rand(1,5);
crazy_y = rand(1,5);
f = fill(crazy_x,crazy_y,'g')
set(f,'LineWidth', 5.0);
```

Output 10.2.5

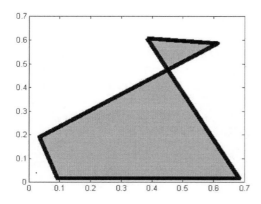

10.3   Loading Images

All the figures considered so far have been generated with MATLAB code. MATLAB also permits loading of images from other sources. Below, we load an image that was saved earlier in `.jpg` format. Two new commands are used. One is `imread`, which takes as its argument the name of the file to be loaded, enclosed in quote marks (so it is a string) along with its file type (`.jpg`). Note that a semicolon appears at the end of the line containing `imread`. This semicolon is *extremely* important. Without it, you would be subjected to a tsunami of numbers, reflecting the vast amount of information contained in an image, even a relatively simple one like the cartoon shown in Output 10.3.1. The image shown in Output 10.3.1 is displayed via the `image` command, which takes as its argument the variable created with `imread`. In Code 10.3.1 we turn off the `axis` for aesthetic reasons only.

Code 10.3.1

```
figure(8)
a = imread('SR_Compat.jpg');
image(a)
axis off
```

Output 10.3.1

"It sort of makes you stop and think, doesn't it."

Here is another example to show that photographs can be displayed via the procedures above. The picture shows the author testing a participant in a study of perceptual-motor control. The participant, who agreed to let his image be shown here, is taking hold of a bathroom plunger to transport it to the platform to the right. The datum of interest is where the plunger is grasped as a function of the height of the target platform. It turns out that grasp heights are inversely related to target heights (Cohen & Rosenbaum, 2004).

Code 10.3.2

```
figure(9)
b = imread('lab_photo.jpg');
image(b)
axis off
```

Output 10.3.2

10.4   Clicking in Figure Windows to Add Graphics, Add Text, or Record Responses

The photograph in Output 10.3.2 includes stuff that is neither particularly relevant to the study nor particularly pretty (leaving aside the author's appearance). It would be nice to hide the section of shelf with the tape measure, folders, and glasses. I use this rather mundane challenge as a way of introducing a useful capability of MATLAB, namely, recording where someone clicks in a figure window. On the basis of this clicked information, it is possible to add graphics or text, as well as to record responses.

The command that makes such things possible is `ginput`. This command is used in Code 10.4.1 in connection with `figure(9)`, which was shown in Output 10.3.2. With `figure(9)` active and `hold` on, `ginput(2)` tells MATLAB to expect two clicks in the figure window. More generally, `ginput(n)` tells MATLAB to expect `n >= 1` clicks in the current figure window. `ginput` by itself (with no argument supplied) tells MATLAB to expect an indeterminate number of clicks until the return (Enter) key is pressed. See `help` `ginput` for more information about this useful command.

When `ginput` is called, crosshairs appear in the figure window where the mouse is currently positioned. Moving the mouse causes the crosshairs to move. When the crosshairs are in a desired position, you can click the mouse so the crosshairs' `(x,y)` coordinates in the figure window are recorded.

In Code 10.4.1, just two clicks are collected because we want to cover the extraneous part of the image with a rectangle, only two of whose corners—the bottom left and top right or the top left and bottom right—need to be clicked for the rectangle to be defined. The two values of `x` and the two values of `y` are collected in `[x y] = ginput(2)`. Anticipating that we will use the `fill` command, we use the two values of `x` and the two values of `y` to define the four corners of the rectangle that we will draw. The result appears in Output 10.4.1. We make the added rectangle white to blend it in with the white of the page.

Code 10.4.1

```
clear x y
hold on
[x y] = ginput(2);
x = [x(1) x(2) x(2) x(1)];
y = [y(1) y(1) y(2) y(2)];
fill(x,y,'w');
```

Output 10.4.1

Text can also be added to an active figure window at a location specified via `ginput`. In Code 10.4.2. we collect just one click at a location where text will begin to be drawn. We tell MATLAB to draw text that has two properties not previously introduced in this book. One is `'rotation'` which is here set to 90 degrees. When `'rotation'` is not specified, its default value is 0 degrees. The second property is `'fontsize'` which is here set to 24 point. When `'fontsize'` is not specified, its default value is 12.

Code 10.4.2

```
clear x y
[x y] = ginput(1);
text(x,y,'Take the plunge!','rotation',90,'fontsize',24);
```

Output 10.4.2

10.5   Saving and Reloading Figures

It took some work to generate the figure shown in Output 10.4.2. It would be nice to be able to save and reload the figure.

One way to save a figure is to use the mouse to open the File menu and go to SaveAs, typing the name of the file to be saved. The figure is saved as a `.fig` file and can be opened and edited later.

Another method is to instruct MATLAB to save a figure using the `saveas` command. In the following example, the current figure, `gcf`, is saved with the filename `'SavedFig9'` and its type is specified as `jpg`.

Code 10.5.1

```
saveas(gcf, 'SavedFig9','jpg')
```

Later, `SavedFig9` can be displayed in the same way as indicated earlier (Code 10.3.1 and Code 10.3.2). In this case, you could type

Code 10.5.2

```
c = imread('SavedFig9.jpg');
image(c)
```

10.6   Practicing Lines, Shapes, and Images

Try your hand at the following problems, using only the methods introduced up to this point in this book or in the problems themselves.

Problem 10.6.1

The previous chapter introduced the `errorbar` function to plot a vertical line relative to points to show the variability of the numbers corresponding to those points. Sometimes behavioral scientists plot one dependent variable against another, and both sets of dependent variables have some variability. Write a program that lets you show variability in x as well as in y, similar to the example below. The dummy data used to generate this graph happen to have the property that variability in x and variability in y both scale with their respective means, but that is just an incidental feature of the dummy data.

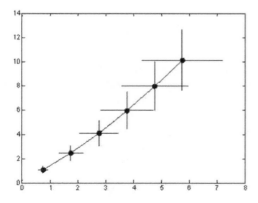

Problem 10.6.2

Adapt the last program to show ellipses around data points. The two axes of the ellipses should correspond to variability along the x and y axes, and the output should resemble the graph below. This problem may take a little detective work on your part if you don't remember the equation for an ellipse. Consult Wikipedia or some other source to find the form of the equation that lends itself most easily to MATLAB coding. The `fill` command was used to generate the white ellipses shown below, which are based on the same data as in Problem 10.6.1.

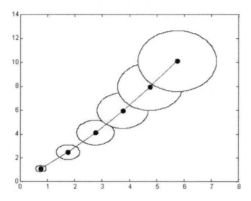

Problem 10.6.3

The Ebbinghaus illusion is a visual illusion in which two circles of the same size (the two grey circles below) are seen to be of different size depending on the circles around them. Write a program to generate images like those below.

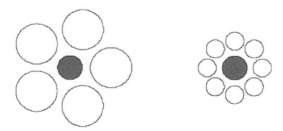

Problem 10.6.4

Adapt your Ebbinghaus illusion program so that, from trial to trial, circles of constant size are shown in the central position, and circles of different sizes and positions are shown around the central circles. Write your adapted program so the participant can click on whichever central circle seems larger. The participant must choose one, so this is an example of a forced choice procedure. Determine the range of outer circle sizes and the range of outer circle distances from the center of the central circle that lead the participant to judge the left central circle as being larger than the right central circle between 25% and 75% of the time.

11. Three-Dimensional Graphics

The commands that are introduced and the sections in which they are premiered are as follows:

`bar3`	(11.1)
`plot3`	(11.2)
`zlabel`	(11.2)
`meshgrid`	(11.3)
`mesh`	(11.4)
`surf`	(11.5)
`view`	(11.6)
`contour`	(11.7)
`surfc`	(11.8)
`surfl`	(11.8)
`zlim`	(11.8)
`patch`	(11.9)
`cylinder`	(11.10)
`sphere`	(11.10)
`camzoom`	(11.11)
`camtarget`	(11.11)
`light`	(11.11)
`rotate`	(11.11)
`shading`	(11.11)

11.1   Generating Three-Dimensional Bar Graphs

It is often useful to visualize data in three dimensions, especially when the data define or describe three-dimensional objects. This chapter is concerned with MATLAB's methods for such visualization.

We begin with the extension of the simple two-dimensional bar graph to three dimensions. In the code that follows, we consider hypothetical frequency histograms corresponding to normally distributed samples of different size. We plot the histograms as a set of ordinary bar graphs and then plot the histograms in three-space using the `bar3` command. The main point of the example is that single three-dimensional graphs can give a different perspective than multiple two-dimensional graphs.

Code 11.1.1

```
m = [ ];
for j = 2:4
    clear n x
    [n x] = hist(randn(1,10^j),10);
    subplot(3,2,((j −1)*2) −1)
    bar(n)
    m = [m;n];
end
subplot(3,2,[2 4 6])
bar3(m')
```

Output 11.1.1

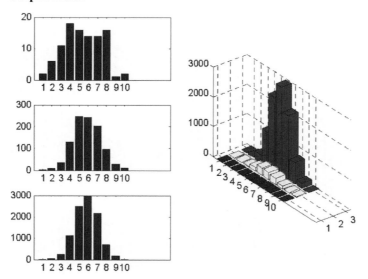

11.2   Plotting in Three Dimensions

The next example shows how data can be plotted in three dimensions with the `plot3` command. The example is based on one provided in MATLAB 's Help regarding `plot3`, although I have added `xlabel`, `ylabel`, `zlabel`, and `title` in the code that follows. `zlabel` is used for the first time.

Code 11.2.1

```
figure(3)
t = 0:pi/50:10*pi;
plot3(sin(t),cos(t),t)
axis square;
grid on
box on
xlabel('sin(time)','rotation',0);
ylabel('cos(time)','rotation',0);
zlabel('time');
title('Upward Spiral');
```

Output 11.2.1

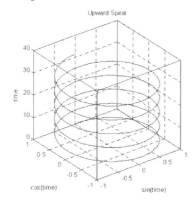

11.3   Plotting "Above" a Meshgrid

The graph in Output 11.2.1 can be viewed as a trajectory—for example, of a hawk spiraling upward in an updraft. A trajectory has the property that there is only way to get from one point to another within it. Sometimes, however, you want to look at an entire surface, the defining feature of which is that there are many possible paths between points. Here the `meshgrid` function is useful. The `meshgrid` function creates a grid of values forming a mesh on the "floor" with values corresponding to each intersection point plotted above it.

The following code, which is slightly adapted from MATLAB's help about `meshgrid`, shows how `meshgrid` is used. In this example, a matrix, `[X,Y]`, is created with the `meshgrid` function applied to a linearly spaced array of 41 elements spanning –2 to 2. Z values are plotted "above" the points created with `meshgrid`, in this case according to the equation in the third line of Code 11.3.1. The `plot3` function is then used to plot Z as a function of `[X,Y]`.

Code 11.3.1

```
figure(4)
[X,Y] = meshgrid(linspace( −2,2,41));
Z = X.*exp( −X.^2 − Y.^2);
plot3(X,Y,Z)
grid on
```

Output 11.3.1

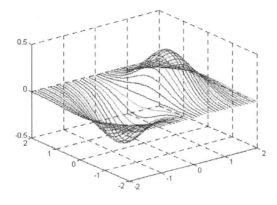

11.4   Plotting "Meshy" Data

The graph in Output 11.3.1 is a series of disconnected lines. You can connect the lines using the `mesh` command. Additionally, and optionally, you can indicate that you would like your "meshy" data to occupy a box, as in the code below.

Code 11.4.1

```
figure(5)
mesh(X,Y,Z)
box on
```

Output 11.4.1

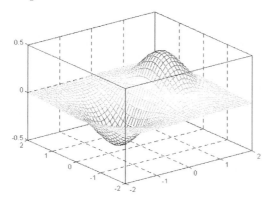

You can regenerate this graph and add points to it with `plot3`.

Code 11.4.2

```
figure(6)
mesh(X,Y,Z)
hold on
plot3(X,Y,Z,'k.')
box on
```

Output 11.4.2

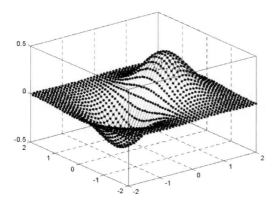

11.5   "Surfing" the "Web"

The surfaces in Outputs 11.4.1 and 11.4.2 consist of unfilled polygons. It might be desirable to fill the polygons to create a more solid-looking, multi-colored surface. Because a mesh with unfilled polygons looks a bit like a spider's web, and because the MATLAB command that fills unfilled polygons in a mesh is called `surf`, I have whimsically titled this section "surfing the web."

Code 11.5.1 is used to display X, Y, Z using the surf command. We give the graph a title ('Surf's Up!') and surround the graph with a box to make it pretty. To learn about properties of the graph's axes, we write get(gca). As a reminder, if you want to learn about properties of surf(X,Y,Z), you can get(surf(X,Y,Z)) or get(s), assuming s was previously assigned to surf(X,Y,Z) with s = surf(X,Y,Z). Similarly, if you want to learn about properties of the figure window, you can get(figure(7)) or get(gcf). Note that the graph shown below appears in grayscale. In MATLAB or in the website for this book (www.matlab-behave.com), the peak to the right is in red (signaling positive values) and the peak to the left is in blue (signaling negative values).

Code 11.5.1

```
figure(7)
surf(X,Y,Z)
title('Surf''s Up!')
box on
get(gca)
```

Output 11.5.1

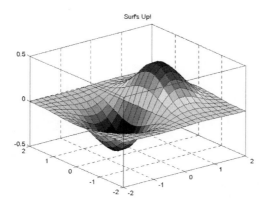

```
ActivePositionProperty = outerposition
ALim = [0.1 10]
ALimMode = auto
AmbientLightColor = [1 1 1]
Box = on
CameraPosition = [ −18.2628 −23.8006 4.33013]
CameraPositionMode = auto
CameraTarget = [0 0 0]
CameraTargetMode = auto
CameraUpVector = [0 0 1]
CameraUpVectorMode = auto
CameraViewAngle = [10.3396]
CameraViewAngleMode = auto
CLim = [ −0.421834 0.421834]
CLimMode = auto
```

```
Color = [1 1 1]
CurrentPoint = [ (2 by 3) double array]
ColorOrder = [ (7 by 3) double array]
DataAspectRatio = [4 4 1]
DataAspectRatioMode = auto
DrawMode = normal
ontAngle = normal
FontName = Helvetica
FontSize = [10]
FontUnits = points
FontWeight = normal
GridLineStyle = :
Layer = bottom
LineStyleOrder = —
LineWidth = [0.5]
MinorGridLineStyle = :
NextPlot = replace
OuterPosition = [0 0 1 1]
PlotBoxAspectRatio = [1 1 1]
PlotBoxAspectRatioMode = auto
Projection = orthographic
Position = [0.13 0.11 0.775 0.815]
TickLength = [0.01 0.025]
TickDir = out
TickDirMode = auto
TightInset = [0.0571429 0.05 0.0303571 0.0571429]
Title = [1168.01]
Units = normalized
View = [ —37.5 30]
XColor = [0 0 0]
XDir = normal
XGrid = on
XLabel = [1169.01]
XAxisLocation = bottom
XLim = [ —2 2]
XLimMode = auto
XMinorGrid = off
XMinorTick = off
XScale = linear
XTick = [ —2 —1 0 1 2]
XTickLabel =
     —2
     —1
      0
      1
      2
XTickLabelMode = auto
XTickMode = auto
```

```
YColor = [0 0 0]
YDir = normal
YGrid = on
YLabel = [1170.01]
YAxisLocation = left
YLim = [ -2 2]
YLimMode = auto
YMinorGrid = off
YMinorTick = off
YScale = linear
YTick = [ -2 -1 0 1 2]
YTickLabel =
     -2
     -1
      0
      1
      2
YTickLabelMode = auto
YTickMode = auto
ZColor = [0 0 0]
ZDir = normal
ZGrid = on
ZLabel = [1171.01]
ZLim = [ -0.5 0.5]
ZLimMode = auto
ZMinorGrid = off
ZMinorTick = off
ZScale = linear
ZTick = [ -0.5 0`0.5]
ZTickLabel =
     -0.5
      0
      0.5
ZTickLabelMode = auto
ZTickMode = auto

BeingDeleted = off
ButtonDownFcn =
Children = [1167.01]
Clipping = on
CreateFcn =
DeleteFcn =
BusyAction = queue
HandleVisibility = on
HitTest = on
Interruptible = on
Parent = [7]
Selected = off
SelectionHighlight = on
```

```
Tag =
Type = axes
UIContextMenu = [ ]
UserData = [ ]
Visible = on
```

11.6   Changing Points of View

I had an ulterior motive for getting the axis properties of the graph shown in Output 11.5.1. Apart from the fact that getting such properties helps you identify the properties you can specify, one of the properties was particularly interesting and important. That property is view.

Code 11.6.1

```
help view
```

Output 11.6.1

```
VIEW 3—D graph viewpoint specification.
VIEW(AZ,EL) and VIEW([AZ,EL]) set the angle of the view
from which an observer sees the current 3-D plot. AZ is
the azimuth or horizontal rotation and EL is the vertical
elevation (both in degrees). Azimuth revolves about the
z-axis, with positive values indicating counter clockwise
rotation of the viewpoint. Positive values of elevation
correspond to moving above the object; negative values
move below. VIEW([X Y Z]) sets the view angle in
Cartesian coordinates. The magnitude of vector X,Y,Z is
ignored.
```

Because Output 11.5.1 contained the statement,

```
view = [—37   .5   30]
```

we can infer that the default values of view supplied by MATLAB when view is not explicitly specified has an azimuth of –37.5 degrees and an elevation of 30 degrees.

Suppose you want to look at the data depicted in Output 11.5.1 from directly overhead (i.e., with an elevation of 90 degrees) and, just to keep things simple, at an azimuth of 0 degrees. Relevant code and output follow.

Code 11.6.2

```
figure(8)
surf(X,Y,Z)
set(gca,'view',[0,90])
```

Output 11.6.2

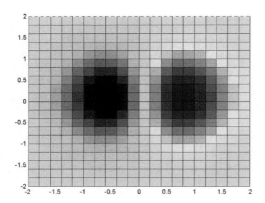

The printed graph in Output 11.6.2 is in grayscale but appears in vivid color in MATLAB or on the website for this book (www.matlab-behave.com). Regions to the left are blue, whereas regions to the right are red. The graph viewed in color looks like graphs often seen in behavioral science. For example, crime rates on different sides of the track are sometimes summarized in graphs like the one shown in Output 11.6.2, and maps of brain activity are often depicted in terms of active (red) and inactive (blue) regions. If you supposed that the left and right halves of Output 11.6.2 correspond to the left and right hemispheres of the human cerebral cortex, you might surmise that this fMRI (if it were one) came from a task that demanded more right-brain activity than left-brain activity.

11.7   Generating Contours

Another way to visualize a data pattern like the one shown in Output 11.6.2 is with the `contour` function. This function lets you see "edges" between regions. Contour maps for terrestrial landscapes typically demarcate different height ranges. The contour map below likewise shows demarcations between low levels of `Z` (blue, on the left side) and higher levels of `Z` (red, on the right side).

Code 11.7.1

```
figure(9)
contour(X,Y,Z)
```

Output 11.7.1.

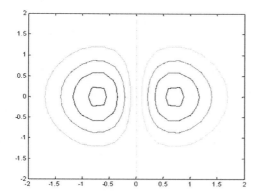

11.8   Checking your Understanding of Meshgrid-Based Graphing

The foregoing examples concerned alternative ways that three-dimensional data could be graphed when z values were plotted as a function of meshgrid-defined x and y values. It is useful to check your understanding of the mapping of z values onto meshgrid-defined x and y values.

In the code that follows, we define an [x,y] matrix via `meshgrid(1:8)`. We leave off the semicolon to see what [x,y] looks like. As shown in Output 11.8.1, [x,y] is actually an x matrix and a y matrix, each of which has size 8 × 8 in this particular case. Reflecting on this result, we are reminded that `meshgrid` generates a distinct x value for every y value, and vice versa.

Code 11.8.1

```
[x,y] = meshgrid(1:8)
```

Output 11.8.1

```
x =
     1    2    3    4    5    6    7    8
     1    2    3    4    5    6    7    8
     1    2    3    4    5    6    7    8
     1    2    3    4    5    6    7    8
     1    2    3    4    5    6    7    8
     1    2    3    4    5    6    7    8
     1    2    3    4    5    6    7    8
     1    2    3    4    5    6    7    8
y =
     1    1    1    1    1    1    1    1
     2    2    2    2    2    2    2    2
     3    3    3    3    3    3    3    3
     4    4    4    4    4    4    4    4
     5    5    5    5    5    5    5    5
     6    6    6    6    6    6    6    6
     7    7    7    7    7    7    7    7
     8    8    8    8    8    8    8    8
```

Next, we use the values of x and the values of y to define a z matrix. For the graph we wish to draw, we want the value of z to be small when x is close to the mean of all the x values and to grow quadratically as x departs from the mean of all the x values (see Section 9.9). Similarly, we want the value of z to be small when y is close to the mean of all the y values and to grow quadratically as y departs from the mean of all the y values. Recalling that mean(x) returns means for each column of x, and that mean(y) returns means for each column of y (see Chapter 3), the line of code in which z is defined uses mean(mean(x)) and mean(mean(y)). We multiply the squared deviations by 10 to make the gradient steeper, and we use surfl to add "lighting" to the generated surface and surfc to show the contours beneath the surface in the final graph, which is here allowed to fill positions 5 and 6 of the 3×2 matrix of subplots. The five graphs use different views based on an initial view generated in exploratory work. We set the limits of the z axis, using zlim.

Code 11.8.2

```
figure(10)
z = (10*(x-mean(mean(x))).^2) +
(10*(y-mean(mean(y))).^2); for v = 1:5
    if v < 5
        subplot(3,2,v)
        surfl(x,y,z)
    else
        subplot(3,2,5:6)
        surfc(x,y,z)
    end
    zlim([0 max(max(z))+2]);
    set(gca,'view',[50.5 v*76.2987]);
end
```

Output 11.8.2

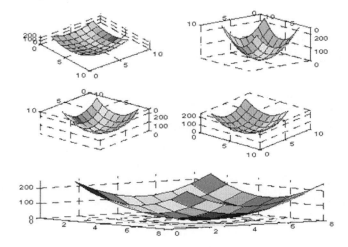

The code below shows the contour map for the surface.

Code 11.8.3

```
figure(11)
contour(x,y,z)
```

Output 11.8.3

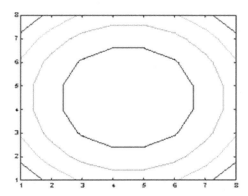

In the next program we create a surface with four minima, not just one. A low and a high attractor are defined for **x** and for **y**, and the value of **z** depends on whether the current value of **x** is closer to the low or high **x** attractor and on whether the value of **y** is closer to the low or high **y** attractor. As in Code 11.8.2, the value of **z** grows quadratically as **x** and **y** deviate from their respective attractors. We use a denser `meshgrid` than before and manually change the view of the graph using the Rotate-3D tool (available when a figure window is active) before copying the figure window and pasting it into a document for presentation outside MATLAB (as in this chapter).

Code 11.8.4

```
figure(12)
[x,y] = meshgrid(1:61);
[rows columns] = size(x);

x_low_attractor = .5*mean(mean(x));
x_high_attractor = 1.5*mean(mean(x));
y_low_attractor = .5*mean(mean(y));
y_high_attractor = 1.5*mean(mean(y));

k = 5;

for r = 1:rows
    for c = 1:columns
        if abs(x(r,c) − x_low_attractor) <= …
            abs(x(r,c) − x_high_attractor)
        x_attractor = x_low_attractor;
    else
        x_attractor = x_high_attractor;
    end
    if abs(y(r,c) − y_low_attractor) <= …
            abs(y(r,c) −y_high_attractor)
        y_attractor = y_low_attractor;
    else
        y_attractor = y_high_attractor;
    end
    z(r,c) = (k*(x(r,c) − x_attractor).^2) + …
        (k*(y(r,c) − y_attractor).^2);
    end
end

surfc(x,y,z)
```

Output 11.8.4

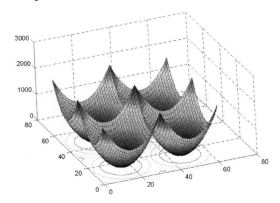

The contour map for the surface was partially visible in Output 11.8.2 because we used the `surfc` command rather than the `surf` command. The code for the contour map on its own follows.

Code 11.8.5

```
figure(13)
contour(x,y,z)
```

Output 11.8.5

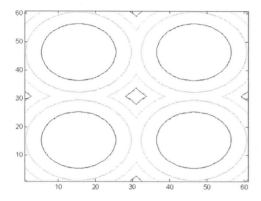

11.9   Generating Rectangular Solids

While discussing graphing in three dimensions, it is useful to consider three-dimensional shapes such as rectangular solids, spheres, and cylinders. You can generate rectangular solids in MATLAB using the function shown in Code 11.9.1. A call to that function is shown in Code 11.9.2. The new MATLAB-provided function introduced in Code 11.9.1 is `patch`, which does the same thing as `fill`, but in three dimensions as well as two. Note the specific handles or properties referred to in the `patch` command below. For more information about these and additional properties, type `help patch`.

Code 11.9.1

```
function drawcube=cube(coord);

% coord = 1x3 front/bottom/left coordinates matrix

x = coord(1);
y = coord(2);
z = coord(3);

vertices_matrix = [[x y z];[x+1 y z];[x+1 y+1 z];[x y+1 z]; ...
       [x y z+1];[x+1 y z+1];[x+1 y+1 z+1];[x y+1 z+1]];
```

```
faces_matrix = [[1 2 6 5];[2 3 7 6];[3 4 8 7];[4 1 5 8];…
    [1 2 3 4];[5 6 7 8]];

drawcube = …
patch('Vertices',vertices_matrix,'Faces',faces_matrix, …
    'FaceColor','g');
```

Code 11.9.2

```
figure(14)
cube([1   2   3])
```

Output 11.9.2

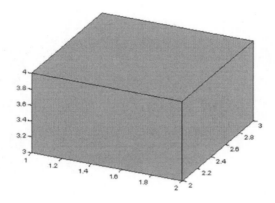

The image shown above was obtained by using the manual rotation tool as well as the code itself.

11.10   Generating Spheres and Cylinders

In Code 11.10.1, we use the `sphere` command to generate spheres at different locations. The sphere we draw has 24 sides. The `axis equal` command prevents the spheres from being stretched in the horizontal or vertical dimension, as would occur if MATLAB set the axis automatically. The view of the graph was chosen after using MATLAB 's Rotate-3D tool (available when a figure window is active). Then the graphic was copied and pasted into the document for this chapter. Note that this is the first time we vary where a three-dimensional graphic is placed.

Code 11.10.1

```
figure(15)
[x y z] = sphere(24);
hold on
for j = 1:2
    surf(x + j,y + j, z + j);
end
axis equal
grid on
box on
```

Output 11.10.1

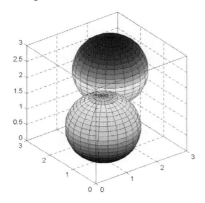

The next program uses the `cylinder` function. We generate two cylinders, one with 24 sides and the other with 18 sides. We place the cylinders at different locations so that a red one seems to sit inside a blue one.

Code 11.10.2

```
figure(16)
hold on
AZ = -37.5,;
EL = 30;
view(AZ,EL)
for j = 1:2
    if j == 1
        [x y z] = cylinder(24);
        k = 1;
        s = surf(x + k,y + k, z + k);
        set(s,'facecolor','r');
    else
        k = .75;
        [x y z] = cylinder(18);
        s = surf(x + k,y + k, z + k);
        set(s,'facecolor','b');
    end
end
axis off
```

Output 11.10.2

11.11   Generating Ellipsoids

Just as a circle is a special kind of ellipse (one whose two axes are of equal length), a sphere is a special kind of ellipsoid (one whose three axes are of equal length). Recognizing that not all axes must have equal length, we can go on to generate ellipsoids. These can be used for depicting biologically relevant forms.

MATLAB provides an `ellipsoid` function. The function returns three matrices, called x, y, and z in the example below. Each matrix is of size n_facets + 1 by n_facets + 1. When rendered with `surf`, the resulting image is an ellipsoid with centers xc, yc, and zc, and radii xr, yr, and zr. The `axis equal` command is used to show the ellipsoid in its intended, stretched form.

Code 11.11.1

```
figure(17)
xc = 1; yc = 2; zc = 3;
xr = 1; yr = 1, zr = 3;
n_facets = 48;
[x,y,z]=ellipsoid(xc,yc,zc,xr,yr,zr,n_facets);
surf(x,y,z);
axis equal;
```

Output 11.11.1

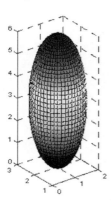

Humanoid forms can be created by using the `ellipsoid` function, as shown in the following two examples, both of which were written by students in the MATLAB programming seminar where this book was developed. Code 11.10.2 was written by Matthew Walsh, and Code 11.10.3 was written by Robrecht van der Wel, both of whom gave permission to have their code and outputs reproduced here. Notice that Matt used two commands that have not been discussed so far in this book: `shading interp` and `light`. Robrecht also used four commands not previously introduced in this book: `rotate`, `shading flat`, `camzoom`, and `camtarget`. Use help to learn about these functions.

Code 11.11.2

```
% Ellipsoid_Man_Matt_Walsh
% March_23_2006

close all
clear all
clc

figure(18)
%thorax
[x y z]=ellipsoid(2,3,7.3,1,1,3);
surf(x,y,z);

%head
hold on
[x y z]=ellipsoid(2,3,10.7,1,1,1);
surf(x,y,z);

%shoulder mass
[x y z]=ellipsoid(2,3,9,1,2,.8);
surf(x,y,z);

%right arm
[x y z]=ellipsoid(3.2,1.4,9.2,1.8,.5,.5);
surf(x,y,z);

%right forearm
[x y z]=ellipsoid(5.9,1.4,9.2,1.3,.4,.4);
surf(x,y,z);

%left forearm
[x y z]=ellipsoid(3.5,4.5,7.1,1.3,.4,.4);
surf(x,y,z);

%left arm
[x y z]=ellipsoid(2,4.5,8.1,.5,.5,1.3);
surf(x,y,z);

%right thigh
[x y z]=ellipsoid(3.33,4,5.1,1.9,.6,.6);
surf(x,y,z);

%left thigh
[x y z]=ellipsoid(3.33,2,4.7,1.9,.6,.6);
surf(x,y,z);

%bubble butt
[x y z]=ellipsoid(2,3,4.7,.8,1.5,.5);
surf(x,y,z);

%right calf
[x y z]=ellipsoid(4.7,2,3,.5,.5,1.4);
surf(x,y,z);
```

```
%left calf
[x y z]=ellipsoid(5,2.5,5.2,.5,1.6,.5);
surf(x,y,z);

%left foot
[x y z]=ellipsoid(5.4,1,5.2,1,.2,.505);
surf(x,y,z)

%right foot
[x y z]=ellipsoid(5.2,2,1.8,1,.505,.2);
surf(x,y,z);

grid on
axis on
zlim =[0 20];
shading interp;
light;
axis equal
set (gca,'view',[107,30], 'AmbientLightColor', [1 0 0] );
```

Output 11.11.2

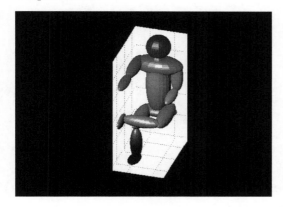

Code 11.11.3

```
% Playing_frisbee_Robrecht_van_der_Wel.m
% March_23_2006

close all
clear all
clc

figure(19)
set(gcf, 'Color', [.2 .8 .8]);
title('Playing frisbee', 'FontSize', 20);
colormap(autumn);
```

```
subplot(4,2,[1:6]);
% Frisbee person
% Order is: Head, mouth/hair, eyes, nose, shoulders, torso,
% gluteus, left arm, left forearm, left hand, right arm,
% right forearm, right hand, right calf, right foot

hold on
% Head M/H Eyes Nose Shou Tors GM LA LFA LH RA RFA RH RC RF
x_1 = [ −10 −9.5 −9.2 −9.2 −10 −10 −10 −10 −10 −10 …
        −8.8 −7.3 −7.2 −9.0 −8.5];
y_1 = [3 3.1 3.1 3.1 3 3 3 4.5 4.5 4.5 1.4 2.4 …
        3.9 2.5 2.5];
z_1 = [10.7 10.7 10.7 10.3 9 7.3 4.7 8.1 6.5 5 9.2 …
        9.2 9.2 1.7 .3];
x_rad_1 = [1 .2 .2 .4 1 1 .8 .5 .4 .3 1.8 .4 .35 .45 .9];
y_rad_1 = [1 .5 1 .2 2 1 .9 .5 .4 .2 .5 1.3 .4 .4 .3];
z_rad_1 = [1 1 .2 .2 .8 3 .5 1.3 1.3 .5 .5 .4 .3 1.5 .2];

for i = 1:length(x_1)
    [xpos_1 ypos_1 zpos_1]= …
    ellipsoid(x_1(i),y_1(i),z_1(i),x_rad_1(i), …
    y_rad_1(i), z_rad_1(i));
    surf(xpos_1,ypos_1,zpos_1);
end
shading interp;
light;

[xpos_1 ypos_1 zpos_1]=ellipsoid(−13.1,3.6,1.6,.9,.3,.2);
left_foot_1 = surf(xpos_1,ypos_1,zpos_1);
zdir = [0 1 0];
center = [ −13.1,3.6,1.6];
rotate(left_foot_1,zdir,50,center);

[xpos_1 ypos_1 zpos_1]=ellipsoid(−10.5,3.6,3.75,.6,.5,1.3);
left_thigh_1 = surf(xpos_1,ypos_1,zpos_1);
zdir = [0 1 0];
center = [ −10.5,3.6,3.75];
rotate(left_thigh_1,zdir,50,center);

[xpos_1 ypos_1 zpos_1]=ellipsoid(−12.1,3.6,2.5,.45,.4,1.5);
left_calf_1 = surf(xpos_1,ypos_1,zpos_1);
zdir = [0 1 0];
center = [ −12.1,3.6,2.5];
rotate(left_calf_1,zdir,70,center);

[xpos_1 ypos_1 zpos_1]=ellipsoid(−9.4,2.6,3.8,.6,.5,1.3);
right_thigh_1 = surf(xpos_1,ypos_1,zpos_1);
zdir = [0 1 0];
center = [ −9.4,2.6,3.8];
rotate(right_thigh_1,zdir,160,center);
```

```
% Catching person
% Order is: Head, hat,mouth/hair, eyes, nose, shoulders, torso,
% gluteus, left arm, left forearm, left hand, right arm,
% right forearm, right hand, right thigh,right calf, right foot
hold on
x_2 = [12 12 11.5 11.3 11.3 12 12 12 12 12 12 11 9.8 8.5 …
       12 12 11.4];
y_2 = [3 3 3.1 3.1 3.1 3 3 3 1.5 1.5 1.5 4.5 4.5 4.5 …
       3.5 3.5 3.5];
z_2 = [10.7 11.5 10.5 10.7 10.3 9 7.3 4.7 8.1 6.5 5 …
       9 9 9 3.9 1.5 .1];
x_rad_2 = [1 1 .2 .2 .4 1 1 .8 .5 .4 .3 1.3 1.3 .5 .6 …
          .45 .9];
y_rad_2 = [1 1 .5 1 .2 2 1 .9 .5 .4 .2 .5 .4 .2 .5 .4 .3];
z_rad_2 = [1 .2 1 .2 .2 .8 3 .5 1.3 1.3 .5 .5 .4 .3 1.3 …
           1.5 .2];

for i = 1:length(x_2)
    [xpos_2 ypos_2 zpos_2]=ellipsoid(x_2(i),y_2(i), …
    z_2(i),x_rad_2(i), y_rad_2(i),z_rad_2(i));
    surf(xpos_2,ypos_2,zpos_2);
end

[xpos_2 ypos_2 zpos_2]=ellipsoid(11.3,2.4,4,1.3,.5,.6);
left_thigh_2 = surf(xpos_2,ypos_2,zpos_2);
zdir = [0 1 0];
center = [11.6 2.3 2.4];
rotate(left_thigh_2,zdir,55,center)

[xpos_2 ypos_2 zpos_2]=ellipsoid(14,2.5,2.5,.45,.4,1.5);
left_calf_2 = surf(xpos_2,ypos_2,zpos_2);
zdir = [0 1 0];
center = [14 2.5 2.5];
rotate(left_calf_2,zdir,125,center)

[xpos_2 ypos_2 zpos_2]=ellipsoid(14.68,2.5,1.2,.9,.3,.2);
left_foot_2 = surf(xpos_2,ypos_2,zpos_2);
zdir = [0 1 0];
center = [14.68 2.5 1.2];
rotate(left_foot_2,zdir,125,center)

% Playground
[x y z]=cylinder(20,50,1);
surf(x,y,z);
shading flat;

% Frisbee
[x y z] = ellipsoid(0,1,9,1.4,1.4,.2);
surf(x,y,z);
```

```
shading flat;

grid off
axis off
xlabel('x');
ylabel('y');
zlabel('z');

axis equal
set (gca,'view',[134,14], 'AmbientLightColor',
[.5,.8,.1]);
camzoom(3);
camtarget([0 0 4]);
```

Output 11.11.3

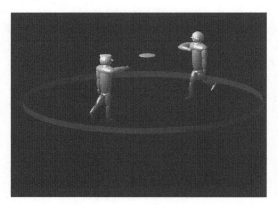

11.12   Practicing 3D Graphics

Try your hand at the following problems, using only the methods introduced previously in this book or in the problems themselves.

Problem 11.12.1

Use `bar3` to visualize the effects of different parameter values on one or more statistical distributions of interest to you (or of your professor). For example the Weibull distribution relates to failure rates over time. It has been applied to such things as infant mortality rates. Wikipedia or other sources can be used to obtain information about statistical distributions. For example, Wikipedia includes the following statement in its August 27, 2006 article about the Weibull distribution: "Given a random variate U drawn from the uniform distribution in the interval $(0, 1)$, then the variate

$$X = \lambda(-\ln(U))^{1/k}$$

has a Weibull distribution with parameters k and λ. This follows from the form of the cumulative distribution function." Show the effect of k and λ on X in a three-dimensional bar graph.

Problem 11.12.2

Draw on the code in sections 11.3–11.7 to generate one or more 3D graphs that show real or simulated data for a behavioral science problem of interest to you (or your professor).

Problem 11.12.3

Draw on the code in section 11.9 to depict a staircase. Draw on the code in section 11.10 to add a railing.

Problem 11.12.4

Draw on the code in section 11.11 to show a humanoid descending the staircase or in some other pose that might be useful to you in your research.

12. Animation

The commands that are introduced and the sections in which they are premiered are as follows:

`comet`	(12.2)
`comet3`	(12.2)
`drawnow`	(12.3)
`getframe`	(12.4)
`movie`	(12.4)
`movie2avi`	(12.5)
`aviread`	(12.6)

12.1   Animating by Whiting Out Successive Images

Seeing things change can help us understand them better and appreciate them more. In this chapter we build on this observation by delving into animation. We first apply what we have already learned about graphics to create our own moving images. Then we turn to some tools that MATLAB provides for creating, reading, and saving animations.

Our first program creates a series of images of a very simple "arm" moving from one position to another with sufficiently short inter-image delays to give the illusion of motion. The arm's "shoulder" is always located at position (`Sx,Sy`), and the shoulder's angle, `Sa`, moves in six steps of equal size from `.15*pi` to `.45*pi`. The arm's "elbow" is located, at each moment, `i`, at position (`Ex(i),Ey(i)`), depending on `Sa(i)`. Similarly, the arm's "hand" is located, at each moment, `i`, at position (`Hx(i)`, `Hy(i)`), depending both on `Sa(i)` and `Ea(i)`, which moves in s steps of equal size from `.75*pi` to `.55*pi`. We plot the `y` values of the shoulder, elbow, and hand against the `x` values of the shoulder, elbow, and hand for each move. To keep the axes the same in successive plots, we use `hold on` and we set `xlim` and `ylim` to visually satisfying values. To ensure that we can see the figure as the animation unfolds, we use the `pause` command before the first `plot` command is issued, remembering to look at the figure window while hitting whichever key we choose to terminate the `pause`. We first plot the `x,y` data with black circles and lines (`'ko—'`), then `pause` for .1 s, and then `replot` the same `x,y` data with white circles and lines (`'wo—'`) in order to

219

"white out" what was just plotted. Pausing for .1 s and then whiting out the just-plotted circles and lines only occurs if want_animation is true. If want_animation is false, we create a set of simultaneously displayed plots which can be copied and reproduced elsewhere (Output 12.1.1).

Code 12.1.1

```
close all
clear all

Sx = 0;
Sy = 0;

moves = 6;

Sa = linspace(.15*pi,.45*pi,moves);
Ea = linspace(.75*pi,.55*pi,moves);

position = [];

figure(1)
hold on; grid on; box on;
xlim([-2.5 2.5]);
ylim([-2.5 2.5]);

for i = 1:moves
    Ex(i) = Sx + cos(Sa(i));
    Ey(i) = Sy + sin(Sa(i));

    Hx(i) = Ex(i) + cos(Ea(i));
    Hy(i) = Ey(i) + sin(Ea(i));

    position = [position; ...
        [Sx Ex(i) Hx(i)] [Sy Ey(i) Hy(i)]];
    plot(position(i,1:3),position(i,4:6),'ko-');
    if i == 1
        pause;
    end
    want_animation = 0;
    if want_animation
        pause(.1)
        if i < moves
            plot(position(i,1:3),position(i,4:6),'wo-');
        end
    end
end
```

Output 12.1.1

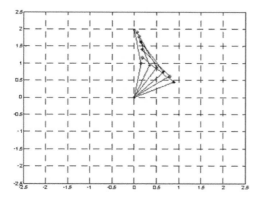

12.2   Watching Comets

Whiting out what has just been plotted is tedious. MATLAB provides better ways of creating dynamic motion. One is to use MATLAB's `comet` command, which displays a moving object along with a trailing tail as it streaks across a plane. MATLAB's `comet3` command displays an object moving, or seeming to move, in three dimensions rather than two.

It is impossible to do justice to the animations that can be achieved with `comet` and `comet3` in the pages of a book. I encourage you to read about these commands in MATLAB's Help documents. You can copy the code and run `comet` and `comet3` yourself to admire the resulting "heavenly" animations.

12.3   Animating by Drawing Now

How do `comet` and `comet3` manage to work as they do? These functions rely on the `drawnow` command. This command, as its name implies, forces immediate rendering. When `drawnow` is contained in a `for` loop with more than one cycle, the immediate rendering occurs repeatedly. Furthermore, with `hold` off, what was rendered before is erased, so there is no need to use a method like the one in Code 12.1.1 where we replaced a black plot with a white plot after a pause. When Code 12.3.1 is run, `figure(2)` appears and, after a key is struck, the arm is seen to move from its starting position to its final position, where it remains until a key is struck again to terminate the final `pause`.

Code 12.3.1

```
figure(2)
pause
hold off
for i = 1:moves
    plot(position(i,1:3),position(i,4:6),'ko-');
    grid on
    xlim([-2.5 2.5]);
    ylim([-2.5 2.5]);
    drawnow
end
pause
```

12.4 Making Movies

If you generate animations with MATLAB, it is nice to share them with others, even those who don't necessarily use MATLAB themselves. Is there a way to save an animation as a movie that can viewed outside MATLAB, say in Windows MediaPlayer?

There is, as shown in Code 12.4.1. This code uses three new commands. One is `erasemode`, a feature that is set to `'normal'` to ensure that the plot is displayed as we wish in this context. The second is `getframe`, which assigns the contents of the current figure window to the current frame. The third is `movie`, which displays the frames obtained through `getframe`. Notice that the call to `movie` in Code 12.4.1 has two arguments. The first, which is obligatory, is the name of the file to be shown, in this case, `F`. The second, which is optional, is the number of times the movie will be shown.

One peculiar feature of `movie` is that the frames being loaded into the movie are shown while the loading occurs. Thus, if you make 1 the second argument of `movie`, it shows the movie *twice*, once while it is being loaded and then again while it is being "officially shown." There is a workaround (or "kluge") for this problem. You can set the second argument to 0 and see the frames being loaded but not displayed again. In my experience, this has proven to be satisfactory. If you do set the second argument to 0 and thereby watch only the "sneak preview," you cannot set a third argument (not shown here), which sets the frame rate for the movie. If it is important to you to set the frame rate (the default value tends to be satisfactory in my own experience), you will always see the movie load first. Thus, you either can set the frame rate and experience a "double feature" or leave the frame rate alone and see the movie once per program run.

Code 12.4.1

```
figure(3)
grid on
box on
xlim([−2.5 2.5]);
ylim([−2.5 2.5]);
hold on
F = moviein(moves); % reserve n frames for the movie
for i = 1:moves
      plot(position(i,1:3),position(i,4:6), …
          'ko-','erasemode','normal');
      F(i) = getframe;
end
pause
movie(F,1) % movie(F,0) is often preferable
```

12.5   Saving Movies

Having made a movie, you may want to save it. A single command achieves this: `movie2avi`. As shown in Code 12.5.1, `movie2avi` has two arguments. The first is the name of the file being saved. The second is the name of the target file. The to-be-saved file name is a string and should have the `.avi` suffix.

Code 12.5.1

```
movie2avi(F,'myfirstmovie.avi')
```

Once this code has been run, you can confirm that the file can be opened and viewed outside MATLAB (e.g., in Windows MediaPlayer or in PowerPoint) .

12.6   Reading and Running Previously Saved Movies

Much as it is desirable to save `.avi` files for later use, it is desirable to be able to read and run previously saved movies, including ones not generated in MATLAB. In this section we first read and run `'myfirstmovie.avi'`. Then we read and run a movie not originally generated via MATLAB code. In both cases, we read `.avi` files using `aviread`.

Code 12.6.1

```
figure(4)
pause
mov = aviread('myfirstmovie.avi');
axis off
movie(mov,0)
```

When this code is run, you should see the same movie as when you run Code 12.4.1.

In the next example, we read a .avi file not originally generated through MATLAB. The file comes from the public domain (http://www.lems.brown.edu/vision/courses/image-processing/Labs/Lab9/) and is called 'track.avi'. In the code below, we only use aviread to play 'track.avi' (which shows students walking on a campus). We also get a single frame from the movie, taking advantage of the fact that the output of the function aviread('track.avi') is a structure (see Chapter 7), which we here call mov. One of the fields of mov is .cdata. If we assign the fourth frame of mov.cdata to another variable im, the subsequent commands image(im) and axis image yield Output 12.6.2.

Code 12.6.2

```
figure(5)
mov = aviread('track.avi');
axis off
movie(mov,0)
im = mov(4).cdata;
image(im);
axis image;
```

Output 12.6.

Note that at the time of this writing, MATLAB only allows for .avi format.

12.7 Practicing Animation

Try your hand at the following problems, using only the methods introduced so far in this book or in the problems themselves.

Problem 12.7.1

Adapt the program used to generate the motion of a right arm (Code 12.1.1 and 12.3.1) so the left arm and right arm both move at once. Save the output so it can be viewed outside MATLAB.

Problem 12.7.2

Adapt the program used to generate the motion of a right arm so one arm or both arms (as you wish) reach out to contact a moving ball. Save the output so it can be viewed outside MATLAB.

Problem 12.7.3

Adapt the program you hopefully generated to create a 3D humanoid (Problem 11.12.4) so the humanoid moves. Save the output so it can be viewed outside MATLAB.

Problem 12.7.4

Write a program to read and run a previously saved movie either with the frames in their original order in some scrambled order. Save the output so it can be viewed outside MATLAB.

13. Sound

This chapter covers the following topics:

The commands that are introduced and the sections in which they are premiered are as follows:

13.1 Playing Beeps

This chapter is concerned with a modality we have paid little attention to so far, although that modality has often captured our attention when we heard beeps alerting us to errors in our MATLAB code. In this final chapter we study MATLAB's sound generation capabilities so we can control, and not just be annoyed or cajoled by, the sounds associated with our programs.

Our first program generates two beeps. We first `close all` figures and `clear all` variables since this is the start of a new program (to be continued throughout this chapter). Then we issue the `beep` command, `pause` for 2 seconds, and then issue the `beep` command again.

Code 13.1.1

```
close all
clear all
beep, pause(2), beep
```

13.2 Loading and Playing Other Sound Files

Our second code example shows how another sound can be generated with MATLAB, a bird's chirp. We pause two seconds, load the chirp file (a file that comes with MATLAB), and then issue the sound command. In so doing we take advantage of the fact that when chirp is loaded, the chirp data are automatically assigned to y. To see how the data of chirp, or y, are represented, we writecommandwindow followed by whos to reveal the properties of y. To see what the chirp data look like in graphical form, we plot y in figure(1). We use the shg command to showfigure(1) immediately.

Code 13.2.1

```
pause(2)
load chirp
sound(y)
commandwindow
whos
figure(1)
plot(y,'k')
shg
pause(2)
```

Output 13.2.1

```
Y       13129    x1   105032 double array
```

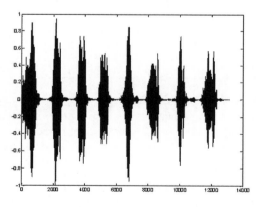

From Output 13.2.1, we see that the values in the chirp file are double precision real numbers (see Chapter 7) within the range −1 to +1 and that they occupy a matrix consisting of 13129 rows and one column.

13.3 Controlling Volume

Our third code example shows how we can control the volume of a played sound file. We first pause for two seconds. Then we load a file that comes with MATLAB, called `handel`. Knowing that the output of load `handel` is `y`, we supply `y` as the first argument to a function called `soundsc`. The second argument of `soundsc` is a matrix whose minimum and maximum values determine the volume of the generated sound. The closer these minimum and maximum values are to zero, the greater the volume. We graph `y` in `figure(2)`, within the first subplot of a 2 × 2 array of subplots, after assigning `y` to `y_loud`. Meanwhile, we `pause` for six seconds, giving Georg Frideric Handel's Hallelujah chorus (or this excerpt) time to finish before playing it again more softly (with more extreme values for the second argument of `soundsc`). To check that the data from `handel` are the same when `handel` is played at low or high volume, we assign `y` to `y_soft` and we graph `y_soft` in the second subplot of the 2 × 2 array of subplots. Finally, to confirm that the values of `y_soft` and `y_loud` are the same, we dedicate the third and fourth subplots of the 2 × 2 array of subplots to a graph of `y_loud` as a function of `y_soft`.

Code 13.3.1

```
pause (2)
load handel
soundsc(y,[−3.25 3.25])
figure(2)
subplot(2,2,1)
y_loud = y;
plot(y_loud,'k')
hold on
pause(6)
soundsc(y,[−15.25 15.25])
subplot(2,2,2)
y_soft = y;
plot(y_soft,'k')
subplot(2,2,3:4)
plot(y_soft,y_loud,'k')
axis square
grid on
```

Output 13.3.1

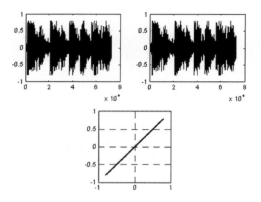

Listening to the output indicates that the sound file is played at different volumes depending on the second argument of `soundsc`, but looking at the output, shown in the graphs above, we see that the data used for the loud and soft renditions are no different. The fact that the plotted data are the same indicates that `soundsc`, at least as used here, only serves as an "external volume controller."

13.4   Staggering or Overlapping Sounds and Delaying Sounds

In Code 13.3.1 we delayed the second presentation of the excerpt of the Hallelujah chorus by pausing for six seconds. That delay was found through trial and error.

MATLAB provides a function, called `wavplay`, which lets you control, within limits, the staggering or overlapping of sounds. `wavplay` takes three arguments. The first is the name of the data file to be played. The second is the sampling frequency of the data file. The third specifies whether control is withheld from the command line until the data file has been played. If the third argument is set to `sync`, control is withheld so the next executable command *cannot* be executed as the data file is being played. If the third argument is set to `async`, control is relinquished to the command line so the next executable command *can* be executed as the data file is being played.

To demonstrate the effect of setting the third argument of `wavplay` to `sync` or `async`, we next play two sound files, first in `sync` mode and then in `async` mode. In both cases, we load `chirp` and then load another sound file provided by MATLAB, called `gong`. Because

loading a sound file causes MATLAB to assign the data in the sound file to y, we assign y to
y1 after the first load command. This lets us input y1 followed by y to our successive calls
to wavplay. Notice that Fs is included in both calls to wavplay. wavplay accepts Fs
because Fs, like, y, is created by load chirp and by load gong.

Code 13.4.1

```
load chirp;
y1 = y;
load gong;
% If sync, gong starts after chirp ends
wavplay(y1,Fs,'sync')
wavplay(y,Fs)

pause
load chirp;
y1 = y;
load gong;
% If async, gong starts before chirp ends
wavplay(y1,Fs,'async')
wavplay(y,Fs)
```

Running Code 13.4.1 lets you hear the chirp complete before the gong begins when
sync is used. The gong sounds while the chirp continues when async is used. It is important to appreciate that the differing effects of sync and async apply not only to the
staggering or overlapping *sounds*; but also to the staggering or overlapping of sounds and
other events. Thus, if you want to plot points, display images, or read in keystrokes using
ginput (see Section 10.4) while sounds are being played, you can use sync. Otherwise,
use async.

You can also control the time lapse before a sound is played with the timer function:

Code 13.4.2

```
load chirp
sf1 = 22050;
t = timer('TimerFcn',' wavplay(y, sf1, 'async')', …
     'StartDelay', 1.5);
start(t)
```

13.5   Controlling Volume While Staggering or Overlapping Sounds

Section 13.3 showed how to control volume with the sound command. However, the sound command does not let you easily control the staggering or overlapping of sounds. On the other hand, wavplay lets you easily control the synchrony or asynchrony of sound files, which raises the question of whether there is a way to control the volume while using wavplay so you have the best of both worlds—a command that lets you control the synchrony or asynchrony of sounds as well as their volumes.

The code below illustrates one approach to this challenge. Here we scale the output of load gong by different amounts in three calls to wavplay. The value of .3 was chosen through trial and error. If you run this program on your computer, you will hear a faint gong, a medium-volume gong, and then a loud gong. You can use this example as a basis for controlling the volume of this or other sound files.

Code 13.5.1

```
load gong;
for a = 1:3
    wavplay(y*a*.3,Fs,'sync')
end
```

13.6   Creating Your Own Sound Files Computationally

The graphs in Outputs 13.2.1 and 13.3.1 are familiar-looking plots of two-dimensional data. Can such data serve as inputs to sound or wavplay? Can we, in other words, *listen* to our data files as well as see them? The answer is Yes.

Code 13.6.1 shows how to generate a data file that serves the mundane function of creating static. Having participants listen to static is often useful in behavioral research, particularly if you want the participant not to hear other sounds in the environment.

The particular form of static that is generated here is white noise. A white-noise signal is one for which the amplitudes of all frequencies within the included frequency band is on average the same. You can create a reasonable approximation to such a signal with a uniform distribution, using the rand function (see Section 4.8). Using rand, you can create a matrix called noise which has one row and n columns, where n is the duration, d, of the sound you wish to generate (d = 1.0 s) multiplied by the sample frequency, sf, which is here set to 22050 samples per second. In the code below, we normalize the values of noise so they occupy the range 0 to 1 because we know that the sound functions works best with values between −1 and +1. We issue the sound command, which converts the data comprising the noise matrix to auditory energy at a sample frequency sf. Finally, we plot noise in the form of black dots ('k'), placing plotting limits on x and y with the commands xlim and ylim, respectively (see Section 9.2). The graph appears in figure(4).

Code 13.6.1

```
pause
sf = 22050;                        % sample frequency
d = 1.0;                           % duration
n = sf*d;                          % number of samples
noise = rand(1,n);                 % uniform distribution
noise = noise / max(abs(noise));   % normalize
sound(noise,sf);                   % play sound
figure(4)
plot(noise,'k')
xlim([1 n]);
ylim([-.5 1.5]);
```

Output 13.6.1

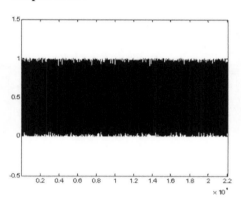

In the next example, we generate a sine wave, both to see and hear it. The structure of the program is similar to the one used to generate static. However, the data file comprising the first argument to sound is a sinusoidal function rather than a uniform distribution. After issuing the sound command, we generate two subplots in figure(5). The first one shows the full sinusoidal function, which is so densely packed that it looks like a solid bar. The second subplot shows just the first 250 values of s, showing more clearly the periodic oscillation that is characteristic of a sine wave. Listening to the sine wave reminds us that periodic oscillations are called pure tones. In this case, because we set the carrier frequency to 440 Hz, the pure tone we hear is the note A4, or "middle A" on a piano. This is the note to which classical musicians generally tune their instruments.

Code 13.6.2

```
pause
cf = 440;                           % carrier frequency (Hz)
sf = 22050;                         % sample frequency (Hz)
d = 1.0                             % duration (s)
n = sf * d;                         % number of samples
s = (1:n) / sf;                     % time-dependent values
tone = sin(2 * pi * cf * s);        % sinusoidal modulation
sound(tone,sf);                     % sound presentation
figure(5)
subplot(2,1,1)
plot(tone,'k')
subplot(2,1,2)
plot(tone(1:250),'k')
```

Output 13.6.2

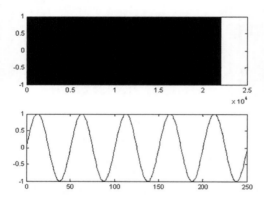

In Code 13.6.3 we again generate a sine wave, but this time let the intensity grow as time passes. We do this by defining a value a, that increases linearly from 1/length(tone) up to 1, with as many steps as length(tone).

Code 13.6.3

```
pause
a = linspace(1/length(tone),1,length(tone));
sound(a.*tone,sf)
figure(6)
plot(a.*tone,'k')
```

Output 13.6.3

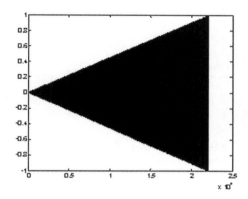

The last example in this section is adapted from a program in the public domain at `http://users.ece.gatech.edu/~bonnie/book/OnlineDemos/SignalsAndSounds/synthetic_music.html`. The program lets you generate a C major scale by defining the notes in the scale relative to A4.

Code 13.6.4

```
fs = 8000;              % sampling frequency
t = 0:1/fs:0.25;        % length of each note
tspace = .05;           % length of pause between notes
fr = 2^(1/12);          % frequency ratio between
                        % neighboring keys
A4 = 440;               % reference note for others
B4 = A4*fr^2;
C4 = A4*fr^(-9);
D4 = A4*fr^(-7);
E4 = A4*fr^(-5);
F4 = A4*fr^(-4);
G4 = A4*fr^(-2);
C5 = A4*fr^3;
xspace = zeros(size(tspace));        % set pause
x = [cos(C4*2*pi*t),xspace, …
     cos(D4*2*pi*t),xspace, …
     cos(E4*2*pi*t),xspace, …
     cos(F4*2*pi*t),xspace, …
     cos(G4*2*pi*t),xspace, …
     cos(A4*2*pi*t),xspace, …
     cos(B4*2*pi*t),xspace, …
     cos(C5*2*pi*t)];
wavplay(x,fs);
```

The above example illustrates that a cosine function yields tones that are "just as pure" as a sine function. Another point illustrated by the foregoing example is that `wavplay` can be used to play generated files, just as `sound` can be.

13.7   Writing and Reading Files for Sound

The final matter to be addressed here is how files for sound can be written to external files and in turn be read from such files. In Code 13.7.1 we use the `wavwrite` command to write `x`, the data file that was created in Code 13.6.4, to an external file. The name of the external file is a string consisting of the name of the file—in this case `scale`—followed by `.wav`, which identifies the necessary file type. After writing the data to the file using `wavwrite`, we read the file using `wavread`. Finally, we play the file that was read in, which we assign to `z`, with the `sound` command.

Code 13.7.1

```
wavwrite(x,'scale.wav')
z = wavread('scale.wav')
sound(z)
```

13.8   Learning More About Sound-Related Functions

As always with MATLAB, there are other methods that can be used in conjunction with topics covered here. Use MATLAB Help to read about options associated with `sound`, `wavwrite`, and `wavread`, and also to learn about two functions similar to `wavwrite` and `wavread`, called `auwrite` and `auread`, respectively. To learn how to record sounds using your computer's microphone, use `audiorecorder`. MATLABs Help will help.

13.9   Practicing Sounds

Try your hand at the following problems, using only the methods introduced so far in this book or in the problems themselves.

Problem 13.9.1

Adapt Code 13.6.4 to play a melody such as "Twinkle, twinkle, little star."

Problem 13.9.2

Write a program for an experiment in which participants make auditory discriminations. For example, participants could perform a forced-choice task in which they indicate which of two tones is louder, the first or the second. Can they ignore frequency differences when they make these judgments?

Problem 13.9.3

Write a program in which subjects answer questions and get auditory feedback that indicates whether they got the answer right or wrong. To make things a bit fancy, change the volume of the sound according to how quickly the question was answered and according to whether the answer was right or wrong.

Problem 13.9.4

Write a program for an experiment on intermodal perception. For example, show an animation along with a sound sequence that either fits or does not fit with the animation. Such stimuli have been presented to infants to determine whether infant gaze durations depend on the match between visual and auditory stimuli.

14. Going On

This chapter covers the following topics:

14.1   Profiling program efficiency
14.2   Opening and editing MathWorks-supplied functions
14.3   Using toolboxes from MathWorks and other sources
14.4   Creating your own toolboxes
14.5   Creating graphical user interfaces (GUIs)
14.6   Creating stand-alone applications
14.7   Reading further

The command that is introduced and the section in which it is premiered is as follows:

```
profile                 (14.1)
```

14.1   Profiling Program Efficiency

The final chapter of this book covers special and new topics that can enrich and extend your MATLAB programming experience. Because the previous chapters were meant to help you set out on your own without giving exhaustive overviews, this last chapter likewise points you in new directions without going into a plethora of specifics.

The first topic covered here is profiling program efficiency. MATLAB provides a function called `profile` that lets you determine how much time it takes for the components of your programs to execute. It also lets you determine other information about your programs. This function can be useful when you want to find out where your program is spending most of its running time. See MATLAB Help for more information about `profile`.

14.2   Opening and Editing MathWorks-Supplied Functions

The functions provided by The MathWorks can be opened and read. Sometimes it is helpful to do this so you can inspect these functions and see how the "maestros" at the MathWorks designed these functions.

Beyond satisfying your curiosity, opening MathWorks-supplied functions lets you edit the functions for your own needs. I do not recommend doing this on a regular basis, but there may be times when you will want to do so.

If you edit any MathWorks-supplied function, I suggest that immediately after opening the file, you save it with a new name to ensure that you leave the original function unscathed (e.g, save `max` as `my_max` if you feel that you must modify the MathWorks-supplied `max` function). In fact, I suggest that you follow this procedure even if you merely open and *read* such a function.

14.3   Using Toolboxes From the MathWorks and Other Sources

There are a number of toolboxes available from The MathWorks. These are sets of functions that serve particular purposes. Several may be of special value to your behavioral science needs. One, the **Data Acquisition Toolbox,** can be used to deliver and record signals to and from external devices. Another, the **Image Processing Toolbox**, can be used to analyze and modify photographic and other images. A third, the **Statistics Toolbox**, can be used for data analysis and mathematical modeling of stochastic processes.

Other MATLAB-related toolboxes are available from other sources. One of the most useful of these for behavioral scientists is **PsychToolbox**, available for free at http://www.psychtoolbox.org/. **PsychToolbox** gives you precise control of visual stimuli. You should be well prepared to use **PsychToolbox** after having gone through this book.

Another MATLAB-related toolbox for behavioral scientists is **COGENT**, from University College London (http://www.vislab.ucl.ac.uk/Cogent/index.html). **COGENT** is a MATLAB Toolbox for presenting stimuli and recording responses with precise timing.

Other relevant toolboxes are **SPM** for fMRI/PET data (www.fil.ion.ucl.ac.uk/spm) and **EEGLab** for EEG/MEG data (www.sccn.ucsd.edu/eeglab).

14.4   Creating Your Own Toolboxes

With the skills you have acquired via this book, you should be able to create your own toolbox. If you have some theme or purpose in mind that justifies a set of unified functions, then creating a toolbox might be useful for you and others.

You can use Help to learn about toolbox creation (just type "toolbox" or "toolboxes" in the Help Index). Through this procedure, you can learn how to create a toolbox and useful adjuncts to the toolbox such as a contents file and a help file.

14.5   Creating Graphical User Interfaces (GUIs)

With MATLAB, you can create graphical user interfaces (GUIs). An example from Mathworks Help is shown below.

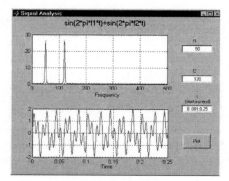

Figure 14.5.1

As its name implies and as Figure 14.5.1 shows, a GUI is a graphic with which you can interact or "interface." You have interacted with GUIs many times, whether from MATLAB or another source. Whenever you click on buttons, move sliders, or type in values in a graphics display, you are using a GUI.

Creating GUIs can be complicated business, so I will not say anything more about it here, except to note that MathWork's Help and Demos can get you started on GUIs. GUIs can be especially useful for getting input from participants in behavioral science studies.

14.6   Creating Stand-Alone Applications

You can write MATLAB programs that can be run as stand-alone applications on computers that do not have MATLAB. To do this, you need the MATLAB Compiler. See The MathWorks website (http://www.mathworks.com/) for more information.

14.7   Reading Further

A number of other sources can be used to supplement the material covered in this book. They are listed in the next chapter. The references are limited to books. I have not listed websites because websites tend to come and go. You should be able to find websites relevant to your interests with familiar internet search engines.

15. References

Cohen, R. G., & Rosenbaum, D. A. (2004). Where objects are grasped reveals how grasps are planned: Generation and recall of motor plans. *Experimental Brain Research, 157,* 486–495.

Dweck, C. S., & Bempechat, J. (1983). Children's theories of intelligence. In S. G. Paris, G. M. Olson, & H. W. Stevenson (Eds.), *Learning and motivation in the classroom* (pp. 239–256). Hillsdale, NJ: Lawrence Erlbaum Associates.

Hanselman, D., & Littlefield, B. (2005). *Mastering MATLAB 7.* Upper Saddle River, NJ: Pearson/ Prentice Hall.

Higham, D. J., & Higham, N. J. (2005). *MATLAB Guide* (2nd ed.). Philadelphia, PA: SIAM (Society for Industrial and Applied Mathematics).

James, W. (1890). *Principles of psychology.* New York: Holt.

Knight, A. (2000). *Basics of MATLAB and Beyond.* Boca Raton, FL: Chapman & Hall/CRC.

Martinez, W. L., & Martinez, A. R. (2005). *Exploratory data analysis with MATLAB®.* Boca Raton, FL: Chapman & Hall/CRC.

16. Solutions To Selected Problems

Problem 3.9.1

```
A = [1:1000]
```

Problem 3.9.2

```
B = [333:-3,3]
```

Problem 3.9.3

```
C = [1:100]
linspace(1,100,100) - C
```

Problem 3.9.4

```
Even = [2:2:200]
size(Even)
Odd= [1:2:199]
size(Odd)
```

Problem 3.9.5

```
D = [5:.5:100]
E = [5:-.25:-100]
F = logspace(1,10,20)
```

Problem 3.9.6

```
G = [1 2 3; 4 5 6; 7 8 9]
H = [11 12 13; 14 15 16; 17 18 19]
G(:,1) = H(3, :)
```

Problem 3.9.7

```
I = [1:10;11:20;21:30]
I(:,end-5:end) = []
J = I;
J(1:2,:) = [];
K = J
```

Problem 3.9.8

```
L = [1 2 3 4]
M = [5; 6; 7; 8]
N = [L M']
O = [L'; M]
```

Problem 3.9.9

```
Jack = [1:3:35]
Jill = [2:3:36]
Jack(1:2:end) = Jill(1:2:end);
Mary = Jack
```

Problem 3.9.10

```
start_value = 1
step = 2
last_value = 80
Up = [start_value:step:last_value]
Down = [last_value—1:—step:start_value]
```

Problem 4.11.1

```
First_Time_Group = [71 78 80 86 91]
Second_Time_Group = [86 91 97 97 110]
Second_Time_Group = Second_Time_Group — 15
```

Problem 4.11.2

```
mean_FTG = mean(First_Time_Group)
std_FTG = std(First_Time_Group)
mean_STG = mean(Second_Time_Group)
std_STG = std(Second_Time_Group)
mean_Diff = mean(Second_Time_Group — First_Time_Group)
std_Diff = std(Second_Time_Group — First_Time_Group)
```

Problem 4.11.3

```
r = [randperm(8); randperm(8); randperm(8); randperm(8)]
```

Problem 4.11.4

```
Vault = [8.9, 8.7, 8.2, 9.1, 9.0]
Uneven_bar = [9.5, 9.3, 9.3, 9.25, 8.9]
Balance_beam = [8.9, 8.9, 8.7, 8.6, 8.5]
Floor = [ 8.9, 8.8, 8.8, 8.7, 8.9]
```

```
mV = mean(sort(Vault(2:4)))
mU = mean(sort(Uneven_bar(2:4)))
mB = mean(sort(Balance_beam(2:4)))
mF = mean(sort(Floor(2:4)))
T = mV + mU + mB + mF
```

Problem 4.11.5

```
Data_Needing_Correction = [23 24 5; 34 35 6; 46 47 7]
Corrected_Data = Data_Needing_Correction(:,end).^2;
Data_Corrected = [Data_Needing_Correction(:,1:2) …
    Corrected_Data]
```

Problem 5.8.1

```
randn('state',sum(100*clock));
std = .1;
for A = 1:4
for B = 1:4
stim(A,B) = (std*randn) + (A^B);
end
end
stim
```

Problem 5.8.2

```
RT_and_PC_Data = [
    390 .45
    347 .32
    866 .98
    549 .67
    589 .72
    641 .50
    777 .77
    702 .68
    ];
Identified_Participants = [];
OK_Scores = [];

for participant = 1:length(RT_and_PC_Data)
    if RT_and_PC_Data(participant,1) > 500 & …
    RT_and_PC_Data(participant,2) > .65
        Identified_Participants = …
        [Identified_Participants participant];
        OK_Scores = [OK_Scores; …
        RT_and_PC_Data(participant,:)];
    end
end
Identified_Participants
OK_Scores
```

Problem 5.8.3

```
clear Identified_Participants OK_Scores
Identified_Participants = …
find((RT_and_PC_Data(:,1) > 500) & …
    (RT_and_PC_Data(:,2) >.65))
OK_Scores = RT_and_PC_Data(Identified_Participants,:)
```

Problem 5.8.4

```
randn('state',sum(100*clock));
sample = randn(1,10000);

% Identify values greater than the mean using for and if
tic
top_half = [];
for i = 1:length(sample)
    if sample(i) > mean(sample)
        top_half = [top_half sample(i)];
    end
end
top_half;
traditional_time = toc

% Identify values greater than the mean through instant if-ing
tic
truth_values_of_indices_satisfying_criterion = …
[sample > mean(sample)];
new_top_half = …
sample(truth_values_of_indices_satisfying_criterion);
if_ing_time = toc
```

Problem 5.8.5

```
number_of_trials = 200;
required_correctly_identified = .50 * number_of_trials;
base_rate = .25; % 1/(number of possible categories)
learning_rate = .15;
last_needed_trial = −inf;     % initialize to this value
                              % to print out
                              % this "bad" value if
                              % criterion never met
total_learned = 0;

for trial = 1:number_of_trials
    if total_learned < required_correctly_identified
        learn(trial) = base_rate + learning_rate*log(trial);
        if learn(trial) >= 1
```

```
                    learn(trial) = 1;
            end
            total_learned = total_learned + learn(trial);
            if total_learned >= required_correctly_identified
                last_needed_trial = trial;
            end
        end
end

base_rate
learning_rate
last_needed_trial
learn
```

Problem 6.17.1

```
A=[1:10;11:20;21:30;31:40;41:50;51:60];
B= A.^2;
disp('A')
for a = 1:6
    fprintf('%7.1f',A(a,:))
    fprintf('\n')
end
fprintf('\n')
disp('B')
for b = 1:6
    fprintf('%7.1f',B(b,:))
    fprintf('\n')
end
```

Problem 6.17.2

```
x = ceil(10.*rand(20,1))
y = ceil(10.*rand(20,1))
xy = [x y]
data = fopen('mydata.txt','wt');
fprintf(data,'%4d',xy)
fclose(data);
```

Problem 6.17.3

```
Excel_Matrix = [];
randn('state',sum(100*clock))
for subject = 1:200
    if rem(subject,2) == 0
        Excel_Matrix = …
        [Excel_Matrix; subject 1 10+(randn*5) NaN NaN];
    else
```

```
        Excel_Matrix = …
        [Excel_Matrix; subject 0 1+(randn*1) NaN NaN];
    end

end
xlswrite('My_Excel_File', Excel_Matrix);
xlsread('My_Excel_File.xls')
```

Problem 6.17.4

```
correct_passwords = ['A1B2C3'; 'B2C3A1'; 'C3A1B2']
allowed_number_of_tries = 4;
number_of_tries = 0;
OK_to_enter = 0;
while OK_to_enter == 0
    password = input('What is your 6 character password?', 's')
    number_of_tries = number_of_tries + 1;
    if length(password) ~= 6
        disp('Sorry, the password must have 6 characters.')
    else
        for i = 1:3
            if password == correct_passwords(i,:)
                OK_to_enter = 1;
            end
        end
    end
    if number_of_tries == allowed_number_of_tries
        break
    end
end
if OK_to_enter
    disp('You are cleared.');
else
    disp('Sorry, your password doesn''t match our records.');
end
```

Problem 6.17.5

```
% clear and then write matrix of passwords
% to an external file
clear passwords
number_of_employees = 100;
passwords = fix(rand(number_of_employees,1)*1000000);
dlmwrite('Passwords.txt',passwords,'\t');

% read in the passwords
correct_passwords = [];
correct_passwords = load('Passwords.txt');
```

```
% initialize values for interaction with user
allowed_number_of_tries = 4;
number_of_tries = 0;
OK_to_enter = 0;
employee_satisfied_with_entered_employee_number = 0;

% get employee number
while employee_satisfied_with_entered_employee_number == 0
    employee_number_known = 0;
    while employee_number_known == 0
        employee_number = …
        input('What is your employee number from 1 to 100?');
        employee_number_known = …
        (employee_number >= 1 & employee_number <= 100);
    end
    input('Is the employee number you entered OK? …
        Type 1 for yes or 0 for no.');
    if ans == 1
        employee_satisfied_with_entered_employee_number = 1;
    end
end

% check whether employee knows his or her password
% print next line during program development only,
% to check that the correct password can pass.
correct_passwords(employee_number,:)

while OK_to_enter == 0
    password = input('What is your 6 character password?', 's')
    number_of_tries = number_of_tries + 1;
    if length(password) ~= 6
        disp('Sorry, the password must have 6 characters.')
    else
        if correct_passwords(employee_number,:) − …
        str2num(password) == 0
            OK_to_enter = 1;
        end
    end
    if number_of_tries == allowed_number_of_tries
        break
    end
end
OK_to_enter
if OK_to_enter
    disp('You are cleared.');
else
    disp('Sorry, your password doesn''t match our records.');
end
```

Problem 7.5.1

```
K = {c{1:2,1}}
K{2}(2:3)
```

Problem 7.5.2

```
subject(1).RTs = [
500 400 350;
450 375 325
];
subject(1).errors = [
10 8 6;
4 3 2
] ;
subject(2).RTs = [
600 500 450;
550 475 425;
500 425 400
];
subject(2).errors = [
10 8 6;
4 3 2
3 2 1
] ;
corrcoef(subject(1).RTs,subject(1).errors)
corrcoef(subject(2).RTs,subject(2).errors)
RT_mean = mean([subject(1).RTs; subject(2).RTs])
error_mean = mean([subject(1).errors; subject(2).errors])
corrcoef(RT_mean, error_mean)
```

Problem 8.8.1

```
% function giving the z score of the j-th element of x
function y = norm_to_z(x,j)
y = (x(j) − mean(x)).* std(x)

% separate program illustrating call to norm_to_z
n = 50; % number of items in the sample
j = 17; % item of interest
randn('state',sum(100*clock));
x = randn(1,n);
zs = norm_to_z(x,j)
```

Problem 8.8.2

```
% RT_and_PC_function
function [Identified_Participants, OK_Scores, …
Mean_of_OK_reaction_times, Mean_Proportion_Correct] = …
RT_and_PC_function(RT_and_PC_Data,RT_Cutoff,PC_Cutoff);

Identified_Participants = [];
OK_Scores = [];

Identified_Participants = …
find((RT_and_PC_Data(:,1) > RT_Cutoff) & …
(RT_and_PC_Data(:,2) >PC_Cutoff))
OK_Scores = RT_and_PC_Data(Identified_Participants,:)

Mean_of_OK_reaction_times = …
mean(RT_and_PC_Data(Identified_Participants,1));
Mean_Proportion_Correct = mean(RT_and_PC_Data(:,2))

% separate program illustrating call to
% RT_and_PC_function
RT_and_PC_Data = [
     390 .45
     347 .32
     866 .98
     549 .67
     589 .72
     641 .50
     777 .77
     702 .68
     ];

RT_Cutoff = 500;
PC_Cutoff = .65;

[Identified_Participants, OK_Scores, …
Mean_of_OK_reaction_times, Mean_Proportion_Correct] = …
RT_and_PC_function(RT_and_PC_Data,RT_Cutoff,PC_Cutoff)
```

Problem 8.8.4

```
% successes_function

function y = successes(n,k,p)
y = choose(n,k)*(p^k)*((1−p)^(n−k));

function c = choose(n,k)
c = factorial(n)/(factorial(k)*factorial(n−k));

function f = factorial(x)
f = prod(1:x);
```

```
% separate program illustrating call to successes function
% designed to check that sum of successes equals 1.
% Ordinarily, k would be one integer between 0 and n
n = 100;
p = .5;
y = 0;
for k = 0:n
    y = y + successes(n,k,p);
end
y
```

Problem 9.18.1

```
x = linspace(0,1,200);
a = 6;
b = 6;
y = (x.^a).*((1—x).^b);
plot(x,y,'k')
hold on
plot(x+.5,y,'k')
```

Problem 9.18.2

```
base_rate = .25;
learning_rate = .02;
trial = [1:200];
for i = 1:max(trial)
    p_correct(i) = base_rate + learning_rate*log(trial(i));
    if p_correct(i) > 1
        p_correct(i) = 1;
    end
end
plot(p_correct,'bo—')
xlabel('Trials')
ylabel('Proportion Correct')
title('Learning')
grid on
box on
```

Problem 9.18.3

```
for lr = 1:3
    base_rate = .25;
    learning_rate(lr) = .02*lr;
    trial = [1:200];
    for i = 1:max(trial)
        p_correct(i) = base_rate + …
        learning_rate(lr)*log(trial(i));
```

```
            if p_correct(i) > 1
                p_correct(i) = 1;
            end
        end
        plot(p_correct,'ko—')
        xlabel('Trials')
        ylabel('Proportion Correct')
        title('Learning')
        grid on
        box on
        hold on
    end
```

Problem 9.18.4

```
for lr = 1:3
    cump(i)= 0;
    base_rate = .25;
    learning_rate(lr) = .02*lr;
    trial = [1:200];
    for i = 1:max(trial)
        p_correct(i) = base_rate + …
        learning_rate(lr)*log(trial(i));
        if p_correct(i) > 1
            p_correct(i) = 1;
        end
        if i > 1
            cump(i) = cump(i—1) + p_correct(i);
        end
    end
    subplot(3,2,(lr*2)—1)
    plot(p_correct,'ko—')
    ylim([0 .6])
    xlabel('Trials')
    ylabel('Proportion Correct')
    subplot(3,2,lr*2)
    plot(cump,'k')
    hold on
    ylim([0 100])
    xlabel('Trials')
    ylabel('Total Correct')
    grid on
    box on
    hold on
end
```

Problem 9.18.5

```
for lr = 1:3
    cump(i)= 0;
    special_i = NaN;
    special_cump = NaN;
    base_rate = .25;
    learning_rate(lr) = .02*lr;
    trial = [1:200];
    for i = 1:max(trial)
        p_correct(i) = base_rate + …
        learning_rate(lr)*log(trial(i));
        if p_correct(i) > 1
            p_correct(i) = 1;
        end
        if i > 1
            cump(i) = cump(i-1) + p_correct(i);
            if cump(i) > 50 & cump(i-1) <= 50
                special_cump = cump(i);
                special_i = i;
            end
        end
    end
    subplot(3,2,(lr*2)-1)
    plot(p_correct,'ko-')
    ylim([0 .6])
    text(40,.2,['Learning rate =' …
    num2str(learning_rate(lr))]);
    xlabel('Trials')
    ylabel('Proportion Correct')
    subplot(3,2,lr*2)
    plot(cump,'k')
    hold on
    if special_cump ~= nan
        plot(special_i,special_cump,'k*','markersize',22)
    end
    ylim([0 100])
    xlabel('Trials')
    ylabel('Total Correct')
    grid on
    box on
    hold on
end
```

Problem 10.6.1

```
x = [1:6].^1+ randn*1;
y = (x.^1.3) + randn*1;
sx = randn(1,6)*1;
sx = .25*x;
sy = randn(1,6)*1;
sy = .25*y;
hold on
for i=1:6
    % plot y error
    plot( [x(i) x(i)],[y(i)-sy(i) y(i)+sy(i)],'k');

    % plot x error
    plot( [x(i)-sx(i) x(i)+sx(i)],[y(i) y(i)],'k');
end
plot(x,y,'k.-','markersize',18)
box on
shg
```

Problem 10.6.2

```
x = [1:6].^1+ randn*1;
y = (x.^1.3) + randn*1;
sx = .25*x;
sy = .25*y;
t = linspace(0,2*pi,1000);
hold on
plot(x,y,'k.-','markersize',18)
for i = 1:length(x)
    fill(x(i)+ sx(i)*cos(t),y(i) + sy(i)*sin(t),[1 1 1]);
    brighten(.95)
end
plot(x,y,'k.-','markersize',18)
box on
```

Problem 10.6.3

```
hold on
t = linspace(0,2*pi,1000);
theta = [0:.125:2]*2*pi;
for offset = [-2:4:2]
    if offset == -2
        a = .35;
        b = a;
    else
        a = .1;
        b = a;
    end
    for i = 1:length(theta)
        fill(cos(theta(i)) + a*cos(t) + offset,…
        sin(theta(i)) + b*sin(t),[1 1 1]);
        brighten(.95)
    end
    a = .3;
    b = a;
    % center circle
    fill(a*cos(t) + offset, b*sin(t),[.5 .5 .5]);
    brighten(.95)
        axis equal
axis off
end
```

Author Index

Subject Index